The Gypsy Kitchen

Transform
Almost Nothing into *Something Delicious*
with *Not-So-Secret Ingredients*

LISA LAMMÉ
OWNER OF *The Gypsy Kitchen*

AVON, MASSACHUSETTS

For all the passionate cooks on the planet—
especially those willing to experiment
and step out of the box to taste the world!

Published by
Adams Media, a division of F+W Media, Inc.
57 Littlefield Street, Avon, MA 02322. U.S.A.
www.adamsmedia.com

ISBN 10: 1-4405-1115-2
ISBN 13: 978-1-4405-1115-8
eISBN 10: 1-4405-1149-7
eISBN 13: 978-1-4405-1149-3

Printed in the United States of America.

10   9   8   7   6   5   4   3   2   1

Library of Congress Cataloging-in-Publication Data
Lammé, Lisa.
The Gypsy Kitchen / Lisa Lammé.
p. cm.
ISBN 978-1-4405-1115-8
1. Cooking (Spices) 2. Gypsy Kitchen (Quincy, Mass.) 3. Cookbooks. I. Title.
TX819.A1L36   2011
641.6'383—dc22   2010039127

Readers are urged to take all appropriate precautions before undertaking any how-to task. Always read and follow instructions and safety warnings for all tools and materials, and call in a professional if the task stretches your abilities too far. Although every effort has been made to provide the best possible information in this book, neither the publisher nor the author are responsible for accidents, injuries, or damage incurred as a result of tasks undertaken by readers. This book is not a substitute for professional services.

Many of the designations used by manufacturers and sellers to distinguish their product are claimed as trademarks. Where those designations appear in this book and Adams Media was aware of a trademark claim, the designations have been printed with initial capital letters.

This book is available at quantity discounts for bulk purchases.
For information, please call 1-800-289-0963.

Acknowledgments

I would like to thank both my grandmothers who took me under their wings in the kitchen at an early age and made me their personal sous-chef. Both cooked with so much passion it boiled over and became contagious. Their love and support was instrumental and influenced my creativity—no matter what I concocted or however outrageous my dreams were.

To my dad and mom, who always encouraged me to go for my dreams and instilled in me early to let no obstacle get in my way.

Thank you John, Freddie, and Lucky for all your love and support.

Thank you to Lory Zimbalatti for your friendship and help.

Special thanks to all the "guinea pigs" who devoured my cooking!

Thank you to the loyal customers who helped make Gypsy Kitchen and past ventures a success. Your word of mouth and support played a key role in my success and encouraged this book.

To all my employees who devoted themselves to retail and maintained composure even when the road got bumpy, thank you for your dedication and hard work.

Thank you to all the ethnic cultures and lands I have been privileged to visit who have welcomed me and influenced my cooking.

Special thanks to Susan Beale at Adams Media Corporation who made my dream possible. Thank you to my editor Jennifer Lawler whose help transformed my original concept into a cookbook the whole world can enjoy. Thank you to my editors Brendan O'Neill and Wendy Simard, who kept me focused along the path.

Thanks to all at Adams Media who contributed to this book from behind the scenes and made this book possible.

Happy cooking and cheers to experimenting!

—Lisa Lammé

CONTENTS

The Gypsy Kitchen Philosophy

*I*f you're bored in the kitchen, it shows on your dinner plate. That's my thinking, anyway. One of the reasons I opened Gypsy Kitchen, my gourmet wine-and-cheese shop, was so that no one would ever have to be bored in the kitchen again.

But if I only sold wine and cheese, that would be boring! So I also search out and sell all kinds of hot sauces, spices, seasonings, oils, and condiments. I even make my own hot sauce, Gypsy Juice! If you were to come into my shop, you'd find everything from my favorite San Marzano canned tomatoes to Outerbridge's Original Sherry Peppers Sauce from Bermuda, not to mention Mt. Vikos Sweet Olive Jam and Roland's Chinese Hot Mustard.

There isn't a boring dish I can't find a way to spice up—and in *The Gypsy Kitchen*, I'll show you my secrets for turning bland nothings into mouth-watering somethings. Here's the thing: many eaters are fearful of trying new foods and different cuisines, but willingness to experiment a bit can turn the humdrum into something special.

That's why I'd like you to read through Chapter 1: "Cooking with Condiments and Spices," before anything else. There you'll learn about how I cook, plus you'll find out what kinds of condiments I use, how I use them, and what brands I recommend.

In Chapter 2, you'll find a glossary of spices. Use this as a guide to help you spice up your own dishes. Don't like thyme, or don't have it on hand? Maybe basil or oregano will do the trick! You can create your own Gypsy Kitchen, using the condiments and spices you like and keep around.

My Mission

I'll let you in on something I feel very strongly about. My mission for this book is to tempt and inspire anyone who has fallen into a cooking rut. One of the best ways to get out of that cooking rut is to invest in your kitchen—and yourself! Although a good cook can make do with what she has on hand, it's even better if you can make sure you have good equipment, clear workspaces, and reliable appliances. If you wish you had better cooking skills, take a class at a local gourmet shop or extension center, or practice, practice, practice.

More than anything, I would encourage you to invest in the condiments, oils, and spices that will turn your nothing meals into something special. Spend a couple of hours at your grocery store checking out the spice aisle. Pay close attention to the oils and sauces sold in the ethnic aisle. Splurge a little and bring home bottles of condiments you've never used before.

And plan an adventure to any ethnic grocery stores that are in your area—Asian grocery stores have cropped up all over, and even in smaller cities, you can find a wide variety of grocery shopping options. Even better, if you live in a small town where there aren't many choices, plan a weekend getaway to a big city where you can stock up on all the wonders you can't find at home.

My wine-and-cheese shop, Gypsy Kitchen, is located in Quincy, Massachusetts and has been named a "Best of Boston" shop. There you can find all kinds of wine, cheese, and pantry supplies. For more information, check out my website at *www.gypsykitchenquincy.com*.

If you don't live nearby, don't worry! Many of the spices and condiments I mention in this book can be found in my online shop—and I'll ship anything we sell straight to your door. Find my online condiments-and-spice store at: *www.drhot.net*. And don't forget to shop your local grocery for things like fresh ginger, sprigs of cilantro, and bunches of basil!

Easy Does It

Like you, I have a busy life, so in this book, I tried to keep things simple. The basic recipes won't have expensive and exotic ingredients. We all have budgets to keep an eye on! Even so, I wanted to encourage you to experiment with new tastes and textures. That's why you'll find that many of the recipes have a "Gypsy Gourmet" sidebar, which will show you how to make the recipe even more special than it already is by adding some of those less common condiments and spices.

You'll also find that I've provided lots of recipes for dips and sauces. Nothing spices up a bland meal as well as a dip or sauce. Keeping some of these around can help you put together a tasty meal in no time flat, even if you don't have much to work with. Grill a couple of chicken breasts, pull out the Chipotle Orange BBQ Sauce (Chapter 4), and you've just made dinnertime a whole lot more interesting! Plus, these dips and sauces are very simple to do. Even beginning cooks will enjoy making them. They're about as no-fail as a recipe can be!

Here's another way to make the kitchen less boring: involve your children when cooking and encourage them to make their favorite foods. This will teach them how to feed their families in the future. Involving family members in the kitchen is a recipe for success and provides invaluable experience. It creates a sense of being needed, opens communication, and teaches a skill. They will have memories of the time spent with you for life. One never knows when one could be sowing seeds to creating the next Pepin or Julia!

A Few of My Favorite Tips

Let me leave you with a couple of tips for cooking as you use this book:

- Opt for calories over cancer-causing ingredients. If you can't pronounce it, put it back.
- Use real food, not processed food. I use frozen and canned foods, but I'm picky about what goes into the bag or the jar, and I read labels carefully.
- Make sure you read the recipe through to the end before you begin.

- Before starting to cook, do all the preparation work.
- Good sharp knives are a must.
- Use the best and freshest ingredients you can afford.

Most of all, experiment with ways to make your tired old favorites less tired—and promise me that this week, you'll try one new condiment or spice you've never heard of before!

CHAPTER 1

Cooking with Condiments and Spices

The best way to perk up a boring protein is by using condiments and spices. I love to explore new spices and condiments from all over the world, and in this chapter, I'm going to share some of those wonderful flavors with you.

Making Your Own

One of my best pieces of advice for any cook is to learn to make your own dressings and condiments. I include lots of recipes for these in *The Gypsy Kitchen*. They're simple to make, plus they're healthier and less expensive than bottled varieties. I also encourage cooks to grow their own herbs and to use to fresh herbs and garlic instead of dried and powdered herbs and spices. I know that's not always possible, so be aware that when a recipe calls for a fresh herb, you can't use the same amount of a dried herb and get the same result. Generally, you use about ⅓ the amount of dried.

 1 tablespoon of a fresh herb or spice (including garlic) is about the same as 1 teaspoon of the dried.

Spices

For those most basic of seasonings (salt and pepper), I like to use sea salt and freshly ground pepper. I keep a variety of peppercorns on hand, including white pepper, which is one of my favorite seasonings! When you see a recipe call for pepper, you can use the more delicate white pepper to keep the pepper from overwhelming the dish. I like it especially for seafood. For more about the spices I love to use, see Chapter 2: "Spices: A Glossary."

Vinegars

One of my favorite condiments is vinegar! I keep quite a few vinegars on hand—wine vinegars, rice vinegars, cider vinegars. Invest in some of these yourself. You'll find they add a quick zing of flavor to all kinds of marinades, sauces, and dips. Other vinegar flavors worth exploring are Champagne, malt, sherry, fruit vinegars, and those infused with herbs.

WHITE VINEGAR

White vinegar is basic vinegar, made from fermented grain (like corn) and water. It's mildly acidic and gives a crisp taste to marinades and sauces. You can also use it to clean your kitchen!

CANE VINEGAR

Cane vinegar is a popular vinegar in the Philippines, where they grow lots of cane sugar. As you can guess, cane sugar is one of their favorite ingredients! It's often used in dishes with sweet or sweet-and-sour undertones.

CIDER VINEGAR

Cider vinegar is made from apple cider and is probably more familiar to you than cane vinegar. In most cases, either can be used in a recipe.

BALSAMIC VINEGAR

Balsamic vinegar is made from grapes, but not from wine (grapes that haven't had a chance to become wine!). It has a much richer flavor than simple white vinegar. Aged balsamic vinegars are worth searching out, as they have deep, complex flavors and a thick syrup-like texture, due to aging in different types of wooden casks. These can be pricey, but a little goes a long way.

A great way to make an average store-bought balsamic vinegar taste like an expensive aged one is to reduce the vinegar in a nonreactive pan on a low simmer, till its volume is reduced by half. Then cool and return to the bottle. This can taste great on ice cream and strawberries, or drizzled over grilled steaks.

RICE VINEGAR

Rice vinegar is vinegar that uses rice as the grain. I like to use seasoned rice vinegar, especially for Asian-inspired meals. Marukan's is my favorite brand.

RED AND WHITE WINE VINEGARS

These are vinegars that are made from wines. They tend to be mellower than other types of vinegar. You can make your own wine vinegar by adding ¼ cup unpasteurized apple cider (or juice from 5 crushed, strained apples) and ½ cup water to several cups of wine. Leave in a warm spot for a couple of weeks. Strain before using. Homemade vinegars tend to be more acidic than store-bought vinegars (7-8 percent acid versus 5 percent), so a good rule of thumb is to dilute homemade vinegars each time you use them (1 part vinegar to 2 parts water).

Cooking with Wines

I also love to experiment with cooking wines and sherries. Almost any recipe with a sauce can be improved with a little wine (and a little in a glass for the cook doesn't hurt either!). Remember, cooking concentrates the flavor of a wine, so start with the good stuff! I always use real wine and never anything that's labeled "cooking wine" at the market.

MIRIN

This sweet Japanese cooking wine imparts a delicious, delicate flavor to sauces.

MIJIU

This is a Chinese cooking wine (also called Michiu) made from rice with salt added. It's used in preparing marinades and stir-fry dishes. Dry sake or dry vermouth can be used in its place.

SAKE

Sake, Japanese rice wine, ranges from sweet (some say cloying) to dry (light and crisp). Though it's called "rice wine," it's brewed more like beer. Sake can work well in Asian-inspired sauces.

MARSALA

Marsala is a very sweet wine used in Italian cooking. If making substitutions, use a sweet sherry or a sherry, not a dry wine.

SHERRY WINE

Sherry wine is a type of rich white wine that can vary from sweet to dry. My favorite sweet sherry for cooking is Savory & James Deluxe Cream Sherry.

PORT WINE

Port wine is a Portuguese sweet red wine. It's made by adding brandy during fermentation. I love ruby and aged ports. They are as pleasant to drink (paired with cheese), as they are exciting to use to flavor a sauce!

VERMOUTH

Vermouth is a wine flavored with herbs and spices—anything from cardamom and cinnamon to nutmeg and coriander. It comes in dry and sweet varieties.

RED WINE

Made from red grapes, red wines are usually used in red sauces. Good choices are Cabernets and Pinot Noirs.

WHITE WINE

White wines are made from white grapes. Sauvignon Blanc and Chardonnay are good choices when a recipe calls for dry white wine. Dry vermouth and white wines can often be substituted for each other in recipes.

 making a wine reduction To make a wine reduction, you heat wine slowly over low heat. As the liquid boils off, the wine concentrates its flavor. A good rule of thumb is: ½ cup wine = 2 tablespoons wine reduction.

Marinades

I also love to marinate meat to give an extra flavor to a meal. Most marinades work best if you give them a couple of hours, so you will often get the best results by marinating in the refrigerator overnight. If you don't remember to do that, try marinating your meal in the morning, then cooking it at night. In a pinch, ½ an hour will do. A good rule of thumb, if you don't have much time to marinate and want a lot of flavor, is to increase the spice. For tougher cuts of meat, overnight marinating works best to tenderize them.

Try inventing your own marinades! Add some olive oil and your favorite spices to a re-sealable plastic bag, add the meat of your choice, allow it to marinate, then roast or grill and see what happens!

Frying and Cooking with Oils

I urge cooks to consume and cook with good healthy oils: sunflower, safflower, grape seed, and, yes, real unsalted butter. I keep a variety of extra-virgin olive oils on hand. The recipes in this book specify either olive oil (and I would strongly recommend you use extra-virgin) or cooking oil. When I use the phrase "cooking oil," my preference is for sunflower oil or safflower oil. Also, try different kinds of oil for different kinds of cooking. For example, Asian-inspired meals can be enhanced with the use of sesame oil. (Try the Kadoya brand.)

BREAD CRUMB COATINGS

Some of the recipes call for bread crumbs, and you'll find you get superior results using panko bread crumbs. These are nothing like your mother's bread crumbs! They're manufactured without crusts, which creates a breading that is lighter than traditional bread crumbs. They maintain their crispness up to twenty-four hours later, unlike regular bread crumbs, which can quickly become soggy. Panko crumbs can be used for vegetables, seafood, and fish and are popular in Asian cuisines. I prefer the Shiju brand from Japan, but experiment with what's readily available in your area.

Sometimes I call for Ritz crackers to be crumbled for a bread crumb coating. These are buttery and delicious, so give them a try!

SAFETY TIPS

It's very important to use caution when frying. Hot oil can cause serious burns if you're not careful. Especially use caution around pets or children. You do not want them under your feet or nearby when frying. Additional tips:

- Do not drink alcoholic beverages until after frying is done.
- Never use a wet utensil or add water to hot oil.
- Never wear long sleeves when frying, and keep long hair pulled back.
- Keep area clear when frying.
- Don't walk away from a pan with frying food in it.
- If the oil starts to smoke, the oil is too hot. Remove it from the heat and let it cool a bit before using.

TIPS FOR STORING USED OIL

- After oil is cool, strain it through a fine metal strainer and discard batter bits.
- Place in a storage container and date; keep in cool dark place.
- Oil is good for two to three uses.
- If the oil is very dark, discard it.
- Dispose of cooled oil by pouring it into empty coffee cans or milk containers and placing in trash.
- Do not pour oils into drains.

Using Cheese as a Condiment

Who doesn't love cheese? But even good cheeses can become boring if we use the same ones over and over. Try mixing it up a bit. Next time you're at the grocery store, instead of your usual cheddar, pick up a cheese you've never tried before and give it a go. For example, I love Gruyère or Compte cheese on burgers—it sure beats American! And try aged Piave cheese in place of your usual Parmesan. For recipes that call for blue cheese, indulge in Jasper Hill, Bailey Hazen, Valdeon, or what is possibly my all-time favorite, Gorgonzola Dolce. When a recipe needs feta cheese, I like to use Bulgarian or Greek sheep's milk or sheep's and goat's milk.

In addition to the old standbys of Swiss and mozzarella for onion soup, I have some favorites that work well and get stringy when heated: Gruyère, Emmental (a Swiss cheese), or Appenzeller (made with an herbal brine).

What You Should Know about Chilies, Jalapeños, and Tomatoes

Because so many of the recipes in this book call for chilies, jalapeños, and tomatoes for texture and flavor, I wanted to share my thoughts on these key ingredients.

CHILIES AND JALAPEÑOS

When possible, I love to use fresh, whole chilies and fresh, whole jalapeños in my cooking, though canned chilies and jalapeños will also work for these recipes. In most of the recipes calling for chilies, Serrano chilies give the best results. Remember to wear gloves when mincing!

THE RIGHT TOMATOES

I prefer Roma tomatoes for most cooking that requires fresh tomatoes. These are plum tomatoes readily found in grocery stores and stand up well to sauce-making needs.

For recipes calling for crushed tomatoes, it's worth finding a can of San Marzano tomatoes. These tomatoes from Italy are prized because they have very few seeds, are less acidic, taste sweeter and have a deeper, richer flavor than other tomatoes. It is best to use San Marzano tomatoes for quicker-cooking sauces as it's not as likely to destroy their delicate flavor.

Hot Sauce, Chipotle Sauce, Chili Sauce

I love these sauces in all their incredible variety! They're all made from chili peppers, but in different ways. Experiment with any that catch your eye. And don't worry: some of these sauces, used sparingly, add flavor without adding a lot of heat. Plus, you get accustomed to the heat after a while. Give them a try! They'll really add a zing to your meals.

HOT SAUCE

Hot sauce and chili sauce are both made from chili peppers and are sometimes used interchangeably. In most recipes, you can use whichever you prefer. Some of my favorite hot sauces are Matouk's, Marie Sharp's, Parrot, and my very own concoction, Gypsy Juice!

CHIPOTLE SAUCE

Chipotle sauce is a flavorful concentrated sauce made from smoked jalapeño peppers, spices, and vinegar. Don't confuse chipotle sauce with canned chipotles in adobo sauce, which is cooked whole smoked jalapeños, garlic, vinegar, and spices in tomato sauce. Add chipotle sauce to salsa, soups, chili, yogurt, mayonnaise, or sour cream sauces for an extra zing.

El Yucateco brand from Mexico is probably the best on the market. A little goes a long way! This brand has tremendous depth of flavor.

CHILI SAUCE

Chili sauce is a spicy sauce made from chilies and sometimes blended with tomatoes. Sriracha hot sauce has garlic, which I adore. Tuong garlic chili sauce (an Asian red chili sauce with seeds, available everywhere) goes very well with Asian-inspired sauces. But my all-time favorite is Lingham's Chilli Sauce. This is made in Malaysia and is all-natural and made from chilies, sugar, and vinegar. It's known throughout the world. This sauce is sweet, spicy, and flavorful.

Asian-Inspired Sauces

I love to cook with sauces from all over the world. Some of my favorite sauces are Asian-inspired, such as soy sauces and fish sauces.

HOISIN SAUCE

Hoisin sauce is a Chinese dark, sweet, tangy sauce made from sweet potatoes, soybeans, and chilies. Hoisin can be used straight as a dipping sauce, or added to stir-fry and other Asian dishes.

FISH SAUCE AND OYSTER SAUCE

Fish sauce is a fermented condiment made of raw or cooked fish and is used in many of the Asian cuisines. Fish sauce is used to enhance food flavor for dressing, curries, dipping sauces, or soups. Some fish sauce can be made from a single species like anchovy and others are blended with several types of fish and added salt. There is a huge array, and varying degrees of saltiness to this condiment, so be aware that not all fish sauces are created equal.

Oyster sauce is basically made the same way but is a lot thicker and has a small amount of cooked oysters added.

SOY SAUCE

Soy sauce comes in many varieties and from many countries. Kecap manis is the name used in Indonesia for soy sauce. There are various types made, some sweeter than others. ABC Sweet Kecap Manis is very thick like molasses and sweetened with palm sugar. This is one of my favorites to use. I also like to use tamari from Japan, which comes in organic and wheat-free varieties. And don't forget to try some double-black soy sauce, for extra punch!

Mustard, Worcestershire Sauce, and Mayonnaise

Practically everyone keeps these three condiments in their refrigerator. They make a nice accompaniment to many meats and salads.

WORCESTERSHIRE SAUCE

Worcestershire sauce is a fermented sauce used to flavor meats and drinks. Many ingredients go into the making of this condiment, including malt vinegar, anchovies, garlic, tamarind, spice, molasses, and sugar. Worcestershire sauce sold in the United States is made sweeter to accommodate American tastes and has fewer spices and is not as complex as that sold elsewhere in the world.

MUSTARD

Mustards are made when the seeds of the mustard plant are ground or cracked and combined with water and spices. I love to use strong mustards in cooking.

Sometimes a recipe calls for mustard powder. I like to use Coleman's for that. I also like Coleman's English mustard.

Dijon Mustard is a strong mustard blended with vinegar and sometimes wine and often flavored with herbs like tarragon or green peppercorn. It can be creamy or grainy in texture. France is known for its Dijon mustard but surprisingly most mustard seeds are grown in Canada. Mustard is a condiment that should be used within thirty days of opening. Over time, it loses pungency.

MAYONNAISE

Mayonnaise is a condiment made from egg yolks, oil, and lemon juice or vinegar. You may be surprised to find that some of my favorite mayonnaises are the ones in your cupboard—Hellman's and Kraft's! But of course I also like to experiment with mayonnaises and have found some delicious alternatives.

Japanese wasabi mayonnaise is creamy, spicy, a pretty light green color, and a superb addition to raw or cooked seafood dishes calling for a creamy sauce. Wasabi mayonnaise can also be used inside or for dipping homemade sushi rolls, in place of any horseradish sauce, and as an especially tasty treat in roast beef sandwiches.

Kewpie Mayonnaise is available in Asian markets and is a product of Japan. A thinner style and lighter in body compared to U.S. brands, it's usually made with MSG and rice vinegar. I often use Kewpie in place of other mayonnaises because of its versatile squeeze bottle and dispenser top that allows for decorating.

And One That Doesn't Fit Anywhere Else

I can't end a chapter on condiments without mentioning this one!

CHOCOLATE VINCOTTO DOLCÉ NERO

Chocolate Vincotto dolcé nero is a chocolate grape sauce from Italy. All natural, no alcohol or sugar added, and it is sweet due to being made with grape must that is cooked down and has chocolate blended in. It can be used over ice cream, poached pears, chocolate cake, and ricotta pie, or in espresso.

CHAPTER 2

Spices: A Glossary

Achiote Powder

Achiote is the red seed of the achiote flower and is used to color many foods naturally. This seasoning can be added to marinades, soups, stews, and turns rice bright orange. Sazón Goya makes several achiote-based seasonings available in thin boxes with bright orange packaging found in the ethnic food aisle of the grocery store. Try them out!

Agave Syrup

Made from the agave plant, this syrup (sometimes called "nectar") is similar to maple syrup. Try it in place of sugar or honey in a recipe (substitute equal amounts).

Allspice

Though it may sound like it, this baking spice (also used for pickling) is not a combination of spices. It's made from the berry of the pimento plant. Also called Jamaica Pepper, you'll find it's often used in jerk seasonings. It's sometimes used in curries and curry powder.

Arrow Root Powder

Okay, not technically a spice, but worth the space! This powder can be used in place of cornstarch or flour as a thickener. It has fewer calories and reheats silky, not clumpy, the next day.

Basil

An aromatic herb (a member of the mint family) commonly used in Italian cooking. Its flavor is somewhat sweet and pungent.

Bay Leaves

These fragrant leaves from the bay laurel tree are usually used dried (when fresh they are much milder). They are used to flavor stews and soups. They're usually removed before serving because they have a very sharp, bitter taste if eaten whole. For a more intense flavor, you can crumble the leaves before adding them to the soup or stew. To make sure you can get the bits or leaves all out again, try placing them in a tea ball infuser (the kind that closes) or in a paper infuser.

Blackening Seasoning

Used in Cajun cooking to add a charred flavor to meats, this seasoning is not just for blackening. I adore using it on fried turkey. It's also tasty when added to butter with lemon juice for grilled shrimp or for fried catfish. I like River Road brand.

Bouillon Cubes

A seasoning for broth, often added to soups and stews to add flavor to the dish. My favorites are Herb-ox brand bouillon cubes, beef or chicken. You can substitute 1 cup chicken, beef, or vegetable stock for 1 cup water and 1 bouillon cube, or vice versa.

Capers

The bud of the caper shrub is used as a seasoning and a garnish in Mediterranean cooking. During the pickling process, the capers develop a very strong flavor that can give a distinctive taste to pizza, pasta sauces, salads, and more. Try them in strong sauces (such as tartar sauces).

Cardamom

This spice is extremely expensive, but it can add just the right note to Indian dishes. It's a member of the ginger family, which will give you an idea of its flavor. Ground cardamom begins to lose its flavor right away, so stick with whole and grind as needed. Try it in a chai tea or a baked sweet bread!

Cayenne Pepper

A hot spice ground from dried red chili peppers. A little goes a long way! It's sometimes called red pepper. Keep some on hand to perk up practically any dish.

Chili Flakes (Red)

Similar to cayenne pepper, but coarse or flaked, this hot spice is made from dried chilies and is used to add heat to many dishes, especially pizza and pasta. One of my favorite types is Aleppo from Syria because it is just a bit hotter than others, and has more depth and complexity.

Chives

The leaves of this herb have a mild flavor that goes well with delicate sauces. I love fresh-snipped chives as a garnish on soups. This herb is easy to grow in a kitchen garden, and there's nothing more enjoyable than snipping your own chives just before using!

Cilantro

This herb has a mild, somewhat minty taste (some say citrusy) that freshens up salsas and many kinds of sauces. Cilantro is the leaves of a young coriander plant. Be sure to keep sprigs dry—they quickly lose their appeal if stored when wet!

Cloves

These are dried flower buds shaped like tiny nails. Whole cloves are often poked into meats to give them extra flavor while roasting. (Whole cloves should be removed before eating.) I like to use them powdered for extra kick to my dishes. Since they are so pungent, you don't need to use many!

Coriander

The seed of this plant is dried and used as a seasoning; the leaf, called cilantro (see above), has a somewhat different flavor. Dried coriander is often used in curries.

Cumin

A strong and pungent seasoning used in chilies and curries. This aromatic spice, with a somewhat nutty flavor, is actually a member of the parsley family.

Curry Powder

This is a mixture of seasonings used to flavor curries and other Indian dishes. There are many different kinds of curry powders, but most include coriander, cumin, and red pepper. They may also include garlic, cinnamon, clove, and other spices. My favorite brand is Madras.

Fennel Seeds

These seeds have a distinctive shape (tiny greenish ovals), a distinctive smell (warm and sweet), and a distinctive taste (licorice). They're used in pizza and pasta sauces, and in specialty baking. You may be interested to know that the leaves of the plant were once thought to be an aphrodisiac!

Garlic Powder

This is dried garlic that has been crushed. It is different from garlic salt, which is salt with dried garlic added to it, which I don't recommend using. While garlic powder isn't the equivalent of freshly minced garlic, you can keep it on hand and use it in a pinch when you're out of fresh garlic. It can also be a good alternative in dishes that cook for a long time, as fresh garlic may lose its zing. I prefer using granulated garlic powder for its texture and taste.

Ginger

This tuber (like a potato) is used in many different forms—whole, ground, dried, candied—as a spice and as a health aid. Many people enjoy it in tea, and use it in baked goods (such as gingerbread!). It adds a mild, but distinct, flavor to many recipes, including curries and noodle dishes.

Greek Seasoning

This is a dry mix, with eighteen different herbs and spices, which complements many other grilled meats and vegetables. It can be used as a straight seasoning or an addition to a marinade. My favorite brand is Cavender's.

Habanero Powder

Buyer beware! Made from habanero chilies, this is one of the hottest chili powders you can buy! If you want a fiery sauce, this is the spice you need to use. If you've never used habanero powder before, start with tiny amounts first. Re-taste after ten minutes (habanero heat can take time to spread). There is no removing the heat from a dish once it has been added. Less than ⅛ teaspoon can be too much for an entire pot of chili.

Jolokia pepper, also known as ghost pepper from India, is now known to be the hottest pepper! It's a little harder to come by, and I don't recommend using it—a small amount can overpower a meal and destroy the pleasure of eating the food!

Jerk Seasoning

A hot, spicy seasoning used as a dry rub on meats, or in marinades. One of my favorites is Walkerswood Jerk Paste. Made with Scotch bonnet peppers, scallion, and Jamaican allspice, it was originally used as a preservative for meats like pork, chicken, and fish. A small amount can be added to scrambled eggs, omelets, rice, or to dough in a bread machine.

Marjoram

This fragrant, mild spice is similar to oregano but somewhat sweeter—from which it gets its other name, wintersweet. It's commonly used in French, English, and German cooking.

Nutmeg

An aromatic, delicate spice often used to flavor sweet dishes. Grenadian nutmeg comes from the spice island of Grenada. I believe it's the finest nutmeg in the world. I recommend keeping whole nutmegs on hand and grating them as needed. Fresh ground nutmeg is perfect for cream soups, quiche, sauces, and desserts.

Oregano

An aromatic spice indispensible to Mediterranean cooking. It's a member of the mint family, and has a warm, slightly bitter flavor. Dried oregano is actually more flavorful than fresh. I prefer Greek oregano for its flavor.

Paprika

This spice is made from dried bell or chili peppers, so paprika can range in flavor just as peppers do. Sweet paprika is milder than others. I like to use smoked Spanish paprika, which has a distinctive flavor (it also comes in a varying intensities, from mild to strong).

Parsley

This is a mild herb that I like to use as a garnish and to add color to all kinds of dishes. I prefer flat leaf parsley, and would much rather use fresh than dried.

Pepper

A spice with varying degrees of hotness, made from grinding peppercorns. For best results, use freshly ground. Tellicherry peppercorns from India are the most commonly used. Experiment with different types: Malabar from India, White Muntok from Indonesia, and white peppercorns from Vietnam. Note: "Pepper" is not to be confused with "peppers," which I talk about in Chapter 1: "Cooking with Condiments and Spices."

Poultry Seasoning

This mix of herbs is used to flavor chicken and turkey. Try rubbing some on your next roast chicken! Most poultry seasoning mixes include thyme, sage, rosemary, and marjoram, so you can experiment and make your own if you like. My preferred brand is Bell's.

Rosemary

A member of the mint family, rosemary has a somewhat bitter, piney flavor and a strong (though pleasant) aroma (which is why it is sometimes used to scent cosmetics and soaps).

Salt

Originally used as a food preservative, salt is now a staple seasoning for many cooks. Use sea salt, which is derived from evaporated sea water, for better flavor and texture.

Tarragon

Also known as dragon's-wort (the leaves look like teeth), tarragon has a distinct flavor and smell, like fennel. French tarragon is preferred for cooking. Russian tarragon, though milder, can also be used.

Thyme

This herb has a strong flavor but combines well with other herbs (you can even make a love charm out of parsley, sage, rosemary, and thyme!) It's used in Mediterranean cooking and complements strong acidic flavors, like tomatoes, quite well.

Turmeric

This spice, sometimes called Indian saffron, has a flavor reminiscent of sharp mustard. Powdered turmeric is often used in curries (and in curry powders). It can be used to give a yellow color to foods.

Yasai Fume Furiyake

A Japanese dry topping mix of toasted and ground seaweed, orange peel, sesame seeds, and spices, used as a seasoning for soups and rice dishes. There are many different blends of these seasonings that are worth exploring. Some include dried fish, wasabi, and vegetables.

CHAPTER 3

Starters

Simple Bruschetta

Serves 4

1 large clove of garlic, put through garlic press

1 teaspoon salt

Juice of 1½ lemons, about 3 tablespoons

½ cup olive oil, preferably extra-virgin

3–4 medium-sized plum tomatoes, seeded and chopped into small cubes

1. In a small bowl, add garlic, salt, lemon juice, and olive oil and whisk together.

2. Combine the tomatoes with the mix and let mixture rest for 10 minutes.

3. Serve over warm crusty baguettes, ciabatta bread, or Baguette Toasties, Chapter 3.

VARIATION

South American Bruschetta

Add ½ cup flat leaf parsley (cleaned and chopped fine), and ¼ cup fresh cilantro (cleaned and chopped fine), then prepare as directed.

Baguette Toasties

Serves 4–6

Toasties will keep in re-sealable bag for 2–4 weeks.

1 baguette (day old bread works best for this recipe)

1. Preheat oven to 400°F.

2. Cut baguette into ¼ inch slices at an angle. Place cut bread on a cookie sheet.

3. Bake 5–6 minutes each side. Toasties should be a slightly golden color.

4. Turn off oven and let Toasties rest for 2–3 minutes, then remove and cool.

5. Serve with Simple Bruschetta, Chapter 3 or South American Bruschetta, Chapter 3 topping.

Gypsy Gourmet

Use sea salt instead of plain salt for better, more appealing flavor and texture.

Crispy Meat and Corn Tarts

Makes about 15 tarts

1 package mini fillo shells (found in the frozen section at the grocery store)

½ cup ground pork, ground chicken, or ground turkey

1 teaspoon garlic, minced

2 teaspoons cooking oil

¼ cup corn, canned or frozen

¼ teaspoon Thai fish sauce or soy sauce

Juice of 1 lime, about 2 tablespoons

¼ cup sweet chili sauce

Peanuts, optional

1. Preheat oven to 350°F. Crisp fillo shells in oven for 2–3 minutes, then set aside.

2. In a medium saucepan on medium heat, sauté the ground meat and the garlic in the oil till brown.

3. Add in corn, fish or soy sauce, and lime juice. Continue to cook 2–3 minutes.

4. Add in chili sauce and cook for an additional 2–3 minutes.

5. Fill shells with meat mixture and top with peanuts, if desired.

6. Cook in 350°F oven for 4–5 minutes. Serve immediately.

Gypsy Gourmet

To spice this recipe up, sprinkle 3 tablespoons of unsalted toasted peanuts finely ground on top of the meat mixture before baking. Or, add to the meat mixture while sautéing:

- ⅛ teaspoon crushed chili flakes
- 1 tablespoon rice vinegar
- 2 teaspoons fresh ginger, grated

Spinach Onion and Cheese Quiches

Sauté 2 tablespoons of thin sliced onion with 3 tablespoons frozen spinach (chopped and drained) in 2 tablespoons butter. In a bowl, beat 3 eggs, then add 2 tablespoons cream or milk and 3 tablespoons grated cheese. Add cooked spinach mixture to bowl and mix. Fill each shell. Bake 5–6 minutes in a 350°F oven.

Mini Greek Quiches

Seed and mince 1 large plum tomato and set aside. In a medium bowl, beat 3 eggs with 2 tablespoons water, milk, or cream. Add 2 tablespoons crumbled feta cheese, 1½ tablespoons Kalamata olives (chopped and pitted). Add the previously minced tomato and mix together. Fill shells. Bake 5–6 minutes in a 350°F oven.

Spicy Goat Cheese and Sun-Dried Tomato Tarts

Fill each shell ⅔ full of goat cheese, then sprinkle with cayenne pepper, and top with chopped sun-dried tomato pieces. Bake 4–5 minutes in a 350°F oven.

Chili Cheese Tarts

Fill each shell ⅔ full with cooked chili. Top with small amount of grated cheese. Bake 4–5 minutes in a 350°F oven till cheese melts. Garnish with sour cream or Fresh Mexican Salsa, Chapter 4, and sprinkle with chopped scallion, if desired.

Chorizo Cheese Tarts

Fill each shell half-full of crumbled cooked chorizo, then fill remainder with a 4-cheese Mexican blend (available at the grocery store). Bake 3–4 minutes in a 350°F oven until cheese melts.

Apple, Goat Cheese, and Nut Tarts

Peel, core, and thinly slice 2 apples. Sauté apples in 2 tablespoons butter till tender. Fill each shell half-full with apples, then top with a small amount of goat cheese and a sprinkle of brown sugar. Place a whole pecan or walnut on each. Bake 4–5 minutes in a 350°F oven.

Almost any leftover meat can be chopped and put in a quesadilla, so let your refrigerator be your inspiration!

Cheese and Scallion Quesadillas

Serves 8–10 as an appetizer

8 flour tortillas, 10" size

1 cup jalapeños, minced (wear gloves when mincing!)

1 cup scallions, white and green parts sliced thin

2 cups shredded Italian 6-cheese blend and 2 cups shredded 4-cheese Mexican blend or 4 cups shredded mixed cheese

1. Preheat oven to 350°F for 10 minutes.

2. Set 4 sheets of aluminum foil, each 15" long, on work surface. Place 1 flour tortilla in center of each foil piece.

3. Cover each tortilla with equal amounts of cheese, scallions, and jalapeños.

4. Top each tortilla with another tortilla.

5. Cover each quesadilla with a sheet of foil 15" long. Seal all edges of foil. Place foil packets on baking sheets and cook for 6–8 minutes.

6. Remove and let quesadillas rest for a few minutes before opening.

7. Serve with several of your favorite toppings: Chipotle Dipping Sauce, Chapter 4; Fresh Guacamole, Chapter 4; Fresh Mexican Salsa, Chapter 4; or Lemon Garlic Sour Cream, Chapter 4.

8. Quesadillas can be made 3–4 days in advance and stored in refrigerator.

Chorizo and Cheese Quesadillas

Add ¾ pound chopped dry chorizo to the cheese and scallion mix, then cook as directed.

Smoked Salmon and Cheese Quesadillas

Add ¾ pound chopped smoked salmon to the cheese and scallion mix, then cook as directed.

Gypsy Gourmet

For extra appeal,
garnish the pasta
with:

- 2 tablespoons
  fresh-snipped
  chives

- Crushed red chili
  flakes to your
  taste

- 1 tablespoon
  toasted walnuts
  or pine nuts

- Fresh ground
  nutmeg to your
  taste

Angel Hair Pasta with Sweet Garlic Cream

Serves 4 as an appetizer

14–16 garlic cloves, skin on

4 tablespoons butter, divided equally

¼ cup chicken or vegetable stock

½ teaspoon sugar (optional)

¾ cup heavy cream

1 package angel hair pasta or thin linguini

3 tablespoons ricotta cheese or 3 tablespoons grated Parmesan

Salt and pepper to taste

1. In a 12" skillet on medium heat, sauté garlic cloves in 2 tablespoons butter until skins turn slightly brown and garlic is soft to touch. Remove pan from heat and cover. Cool for 30 minutes.

2. Peel and coarsely chop cooled garlic.

3. In 12" skillet on low heat, melt remainder of butter. Add chopped garlic and sauté 1–2 minutes. Add stock and sugar (if desired) to pan. Simmer 3–4 minutes. Add cream and simmer additional 3–4 minutes, stirring occasionally.

4. As sauce is cooking, cook pasta per manufacturer's instructions. *Note*: It's important to make sauce before cooking angel hair pasta due to quick cooking time of pasta.

5. Add drained cooked pasta to garlic-cream mixture. Add ricotta and toss. Salt and pepper to taste. Serve.

Kielbasa with Sweet and Spicy Relish

Serves 6–8 as an appetizer

⅓ cup hot sweet pepper relish or substitute ⅓ cup sweet relish with ½ teaspoon cayenne pepper

⅓ cup Dijon mustard

3 cups water

½ teaspoon salt

1 pound kielbasa

1. In a small bowl, whisk together relish and mustard. Set aside.

2. In a 10" skillet, bring water and salt to a boil on medium heat.

3. Add kielbasa and simmer 10–15 minutes.

4. Thinly slice cooled kielbasa and serve with relish-and-mustard sauce.

Sauce can be used for bratwurst, hot dogs, sausages, and knockwurst.

Gypsy Gourmet

For more flavor, substitute 1 can of beer for 1½ cups water and boil as directed. You can also grill after simmering. Simmering sausages in beer or water prior to grilling makes for a juicy sausage each time.

All recipes may be doubled if you need to make more than 6 servings. You can also use smaller crescent rolls (the kind that come in a package of 8). Reduce the filling proportionately.

Grand Crescent Rolls

6 servings

1 package crescent rolls, big and flaky (makes 6 dinner rolls)

1. Preheat oven per crescent roll manufacturer's instruction.

2. Stuff with choice of fillings below. Each recipe will fill 6 rolls.

3. For each filling, use a small bowl to blend the ingredients. Spread a spoonful of filling inside of each roll, fold per manufacturer's direction, and then bake as directed.

VARIATIONS

Spinach Goat Cheese Filling

¼ cup cooked spinach, drained
3 tablespoons soft goat cheese
1 tablespoon grated Parmesan or Romano cheese
¼ teaspoon garlic powder
¼ teaspoon grated nutmeg

Raspberry-Chipotle Filling

3 tablespoons raspberry preserves
½ teaspoon chipotle sauce

Orange Marmalade Basil Filling

3 tablespoons orange marmalade
1½ tablespoons chopped basil

Herb Butter Filling

2 tablespoons butter, melted
1 clove garlic, put through press
1½ teaspoons chopped rosemary
1 tablespoon grated Parmesan cheese

Fig, Goat Cheese, and Walnut Filling

1 tablespoon chopped walnuts
3 tablespoons soft goat cheese
3 tablespoons fig preserves

Cinnamon Brown Sugar Filling

¼ cup packed brown sugar
1 tablespoon, plus 2 teaspoons cinnamon
¼ teaspoon cayenne pepper

Recipe for nachos can be doubled or even tripled it you are having a party. You can keep warmed toppings warm in a crockpot. You can melt cheese on larger batches of nachos on cookie sheets in an oven at 375°F for 7–10 minutes.

Party Time Nachos

Serves 2–4

3–4 cups plain nacho chips

1½ cups 4-cheese Mexican blend or 6-cheese blend

1 cup Lemon Garlic Sour Cream, Chapter 4, or plain sour cream

1 cup Fresh Mexican Salsa, Chapter 4, or your favorite salsa

Your choice of toppings (see list)

1. Place nachos on a large microwave-safe dish. Sprinkle cheese evenly over nachos. Melt in microwave on high for 1 minute, then continue cooking in 30-second intervals until cheese is melted.

2. Add sour cream and salsa, plus all of your favorite toppings (set them up before melting the cheese):

 Choose nacho toppings from this list. Try some you've never tried before!

- 2 jalapeños, sliced thin
- 2 scallions, white and green parts sliced thin
- 2 tablespoons onion, chopped (preferably red onion)
- 2 tablespoons pitted black olives (chopped)
- ½ cup chopped tomatoes
- ½ cup Fresh Guacamole, Chapter 4
- ½ cup Black Bean Dip, Chapter 4, warmed
- ½ cup Three Bean and Beef Chili, Chapter 7, warmed
- ¼ cup Gypsy Dip, Chapter 4

Black Eyed Peas with Bacon and Onions

Serves 4–6

3 slices bacon

2 cloves garlic, put through press

1 large onion, chopped

2 15-ounce cans black-eyed peas, drained and rinsed, or 4 cups frozen

½ cup chicken stock

1 teaspoon hot sauce

Salt and pepper to taste

1. In a 10" skillet, sauté bacon on medium heat till crispy.

2. Add garlic and onions and sauté 3–4 minutes.

3. Add peas, stock, and hot sauce. Reduce heat to low and simmer 8–10 minutes.

4. Season with salt and pepper to taste and serve.

 Mustard or turnip greens can be substituted for collard greens.

Collard Greens

Serves 2–4

2 pieces bacon or pork fat back

1 large onion, chopped

3–4 cloves garlic, put through press

1 pound collard greens, chopped

¾ cup chicken stock

1 tablespoon vinegar

4–5 dashes hot sauce or ¼ teaspoon cayenne pepper

1. Sauté bacon in 10" skillet on medium heat till crispy.

2. Drain bacon. Crumble and return to pan.

3. Add onion and garlic to bacon grease and cook till tender.

4. Add in greens, stock, vinegar, and hot sauce.

5. Reduce heat and simmer 10–15 minutes till no liquid remains in pan.

Fried Calamari

Serves 4

½ cup all-purpose flour

1 teaspoon pepper

½ teaspoon salt

1 pound squid rings and tentacles, cleaned

1–2 cups cooking oil

1. Mix flour, pepper, and salt together in a small bowl.

2. Coat squid in dry flour batter and set aside.

3. In a medium nonstick skillet, add oil to about ⅓ full. Turn to medium-high heat. Oil is ready for frying when small amount of batter added to oil sizzles.

4. Fry squid in small batches, cooking 1–2 minutes till golden. Use slotted spoon to lift from pan; drain on paper-towel-lined plate.

5. Serve immediately with your choice of aioli sauce or Red Sauce, Chapter 4.

Gypsy Gourmet

When cooking seafood or other delicate meats, use white pepper instead of black pepper to keep from overwhelming the dish.

Rangoons can be made assembled a day in advance as long as wax or parchment paper is placed between the pieces to keep them separated. Then cook as directed.

Gypsy Gourmet

To upgrade this recipe, add to the shrimp-cream cheese mixture:

- 1 tablespoon grated carrot (for sweetness and color in the filling)
- 1/8 teaspoon ground nutmeg
- 1 tablespoon fresh-snipped chives

Fried Shrimp Rangoon with Dipping Sauce

Makes 22–24 pieces

6 ounces whipped or soft cream cheese

1/4 teaspoon pepper

1/4 teaspoon salt

1/2 teaspoon garlic powder

5 ounces cooked shrimp, drained, dried, and chopped (lobster or crab can be substituted)

1 package of wonton wrappers

Small bowl of water

1 cup cooking oil

1 recipe Sweet Chili Dipping Sauce, Chapter 4, or Ginger Dipping Sauce, Chapter 4

1. Blend cream cheese, pepper, salt, and garlic powder in a medium bowl. Add shrimp and mix thoroughly.

2. Place a wonton wrapper in your palm. Place a teaspoon of shrimp batter in center of wrapper.

3. Dip fingers in water and moisten the inside of one side of the wrapper. Fold wrapper into a triangle shape and pinch sides together. Set aside until all pieces are assembled. Cover in plastic wrap and refrigerate, if not cooking immediately.

4. To fry, place oil in a 10" skillet set on medium heat. To tell when oil is ready, place an empty wonton wrapper in the oil. The oil is ready when the wrapper gets crispy and floats to the top.

5. Fry in batches of 5–6 at a time, for 2–3 minutes. Drain on a paper-towel-lined plate.

6. Serve with Sweet Chili Dipping Sauce, Chapter 4, or Ginger Dipping Sauce, Chapter 4.

picking a wonton wrapper For best results with this recipe, use yellow wonton wrappers (available at Asian markets). These wonton skins contain more egg and crisp up better when frying. The regular wonton wrappers readily available at grocery stores are very thick and doughy and contain no or little egg. They are better suited for boiling or steaming.

Homemade Mozzarella Sticks

Serves 4–6 as appetizer

1 pound block mozzarella

¼ cup all-purpose flour

2 eggs

3 tablespoons water

1½ cups bread crumbs

1 tablespoon oregano

½ teaspoon salt

1 teaspoon garlic powder

2–2½ cups cooking oil

1 recipe Red Sauce, Chapter 4

1. Cut mozzarella into finger-sized pieces. Set aside. Place flour in small bowl and set aside. Whisk egg and water together in a small bowl and set aside.

2. Combine bread crumbs, oregano, salt, and garlic powder in a medium-sized bowl or bag and set aside.

3. Coat mozzarella sticks in flour, then dip into egg wash, then coat with bread crumb mixture. Set aside.

4. Heat oil in 10" skillet or sauté pan (it should be about ⅓ full). Oil is ready for frying when small portion of a mozzarella stick placed in oil as a test sizzles. Fry 4–5 sticks at a time. Do not overcrowd the skillet. Sticks cook in 1–2 minutes and are done when crumbs turn golden brown. Drain on paper-towel-lined plate, then transfer to serving dish and serve immediately with Red Sauce, Chapter 4.

Marinated Feta Cheese

Serves 4–6

½ pound firm feta cheese, rinsed and cut into 1" cubes.

1 cup olive oil, preferably extra-virgin

5–7 fresh thyme sprigs

8–10 whole black peppercorns

¼ teaspoon red chili flakes

1. Place cheese in 16-ounce jar with a lid.

2. Warm olive oil in pan on medium heat for 4–5 minutes.

3. Add thyme, peppercorns, and chili flakes to oil. Turn heat off. Cool for 10–15 minutes, until oil is slightly warm to the touch but not hot.

4. Pour oil over cheese in jar, being sure to cover cheese completely.

5. Cover and refrigerate for at least 6 hours or up to several days. Cheese will keep in refrigerator for up to a month.

6. Serve at room temperature.

7. Spread the marinated cheese on warm crusty bread, or over chopped, fresh, garden heirloom tomatoes.

Lemon Olives

Yields 1–2 pounds

1–2 pounds assorted olives

2 tablespoons olive oil

Zest from 2 whole lemons

2 tablespoons lemon juice

⅛ teaspoon salt

¼ teaspoon garlic, put through press

Few pieces of lemon peel (optional)

1. Put olives in a medium-size bowl. Add other ingredients and mix.

2. Marinate in refrigerator at least 30 minutes. Will keep covered in refrigerator up to 3 days.

3. Use to garnish cold-cut trays, antipasto salads, or serve in small dishes around a room during a cocktail party.

Marinated Portabella Caps with Crumb Topping

Serves 4

Portabella caps can be placed in marinade a few days in advance and cooked when needed.

5 large portabella mushroom caps

2 tablespoons olive oil, preferably extra-virgin

½ teaspoon salt

1 teaspoon garlic, minced

½ stick butter

3 tablespoons blue cheese, such as Gorgonzola Dolce, Roquefort, or Stilton

¼ cup bread crumbs

1. Place mushrooms face down in microwave-safe dish and cover. Cook on high in microwave for 5 minutes. Let rest for 10 minutes, then uncover and cool.

2. Remove stems from portabellas and set stems aside. Squeeze out excess moisture from each portabella cap. Return 4 portabellas to dish, reserving the 5th.

3. In a food processor, combine the portabella stems, the 5th portabella cap, oil, salt, and garlic. Purée.

4. Pour marinade over portabella caps and let sit for ½ hour.

5. Preheat oven to 400°F.

6. Remove portabellas from marinade and place in 10" pie plate or casserole. Reserve marinade.

continued on following page

Gypsy Gourmet

To add a special flavor to this recipe, add ½ cup sherry, port, or sweet Marsala wine to the marinade. I prefer Savory & James Deluxe Cream Sherry.

7. In a 10" skilled on low heat, melt butter. Add reserved marinade and cook for 3–5 minutes. Add blue cheese till melted.

8. Pour cheese-and-marinade mixture over each portabella cap, then cover with bread crumbs.

9. Bake 8–10 minutes and serve while warm.

VARIATION

Grill Method

Before cooking portabellas in microwave, cut core so that it equals level of cap. Skip extra mushrooms, bread crumbs, butter. Marinade per instructions and grill on medium heat for 5–7 minutes. Blue cheese dollops can be placed on top inside of each cap when coming off grill.

Tomato Cucumber Salad

Serves 2–4

3–4 cucumbers, peeled and cut to desired size

2–3 tomatoes, chopped

1 small onion, chopped

2 tablespoon vinegar

¼ cup olive oil

2 cloves garlic, put through press

½ teaspoon salt

Dash pepper

1. In a medium bowl, add cucumbers, tomatoes, and onion. Set aside.

2. In a small bowl, whisk together vinegar, oil, garlic, salt, and pepper.

3. Cover vegetables and mix.

4. Let sit for 30 minutes, then mix again before serving.

Sweet and Spicy Ginger Wings

Serves 6–8

4–5 pounds large fresh chicken wings, cleaned

3 tablespoons soy sauce

1½ teaspoons salt

4 tablespoons garlic, puréed

4 tablespoons fresh ginger, puréed

3 tablespoons oil, preferably toasted sesame oil

1 recipe Sweet and Spicy Sauce, Chapter 4

1. Combine all ingredients in a large gallon-sized, re-sealable bag. Add wings. Seal bag and gently turn bag over several times to coat all wings.

2. Marinate at least 6 hours and up to 2 days in the refrigerator, turning the bag a few times.

3. Preheat oven to 400°F. Line 1 large lipped cookie sheet or baking sheet with foil, then brush the foil with oil. Place wings on the sheet, making sure the wings don't touch.

4. Bake on top rack for 40–45 minutes till golden crispy, turning once.

5. Serve with Sweet and Spicy Sauce (Chapter 4).

Gypsy Gourmet

For an extra kick, add 1 teaspoon MSG to the marinade (I like the Ajinomoto brand), and garnish the finished wings with red and green jalapeño slices.

Dips, Spreads, and Sauces

Cheese Dip

Serves 2

1 cup Mexican cheese blend or 6-cheese blend, grated

¼ cup milk or half-and-half

1 scallion chopped (optional)

1. In a microwave-safe medium-size bowl, add cheese, milk, and scallion if desired. Microwave on high 1–1½ minutes. Stir.

2. Serve immediately. Use as a dip for your favorite chips or tortillas. Re-heat each time it gets cold, or it is not a dip, it's a cheese mass!

VARIATION

Cheese-Chorizo Dip

Add 2–3 tablespoons ground chorizo to the dip. You can also use chopped pepperoni or bacon bits.

Sweet Chili Dipping Sauce

Serves 1–2

Juice of 1 lime, about 2 tablespoons

2 tablespoons sugar

¾ teaspoon chili sauce

1½ teaspoons soy, tamari, or fish sauce

1. Combine ingredients in small bowl. Can be stored in sealed container in refrigerator for up to 2 weeks.

2. Serve with Fried Shrimp Rangoon, Chapter 3.

Spinach Dip

Makes about 1½ cups

½ cup frozen spinach, thawed, squeezed dry, and chopped

½ teaspoon salt

½ cup plain yogurt or sour cream

½ cup mayonnaise

1 teaspoon garlic powder

1 tablespoon, plus 1 teaspoon lemon juice

1. Combine ingredients in a small bowl. Let mixture rest for 15 minutes.

2. Serve with a vegetable crudités tray (see list).

VARIATIONS

Stuffed Celery

Place spinach dip in celery sticks.

Deviled Spinach Eggs

Remove the yolks from 12 hard-boiled eggs and fill with spinach dip. Garnish with smoked paprika, fresh snipped chives, or chopped fresh parsley.

Gypsy Gourmet

To fancy this recipe up, serve the dip in a small bread bowl and garnish with chopped walnuts, toasted almond slivers, or paprika.

vegetable crudités tray

Clean and cut to desired size any of the following:

- Baby carrots
- Celery sticks
- Grape tomatoes
- Pea pods
- Broccoli and cauliflower florets
- Green beans
- Zucchini sticks

Ginger Dipping Sauce

Makes ¼ cup

1 tablespoon soy sauce

2 teaspoons fresh ginger, grated

1 scallion, thinly chopped (white and green parts)

1 tablespoon water

Gypsy Gourmet

To add extra flavor to this ginger sauce, add:

• 1 tablespoon toasted sesame oil

• 2 tablespoons Mirin cooking wine

1. Combine all ingredients in a small bowl. Will keep for 3–4 days in covered container in refrigerator.

2. Serve with Fried Shrimp Rangoon, Chapter 3.

Herb Butters

*Each recipe makes ⅓ cup, enough to do 12 rolls,
2 loaves bread, or 3–4 cups vegetables*

Before warming
bread, brush top
with herb butter,
then sprinkle with
cheese.

For all of the variations (provided below), heat butter, herbs,
and spices in small microwave-safe bowl for 45 seconds to
1 minute on high. If needed, heat an additional 30–40 seconds till completely melted.

For best results, use unsalted butter.

Use as dipping sauces. Or, chill 45 minutes and use as
a spread for bread, rolls, and buns. A dollop of chilled herb
butters can be served on cooked vegetables, such as summer squash, zucchini, or boiled potatoes, or served with fish
dishes.

VARIATIONS

Herb Butter

3 tablespoons butter
½ teaspoon thyme
Pinch of salt (omit if using salted butter)
1 tablespoon grated Parmesan cheese or other grated hard cheese

Rosemary Garlic Butter

3 tablespoons butter
1 clove garlic, put through press
1 teaspoon rosemary, minced fine
Pinch of salt (omit if using salted butter)
1 tablespoon grated Parmesan cheese or other grated hard cheese

continued on following page

Thyme Garlic Butter

3 tablespoons butter

1 clove garlic, put through press

1 teaspoon fresh thyme, stems off

Pinch of salt (omit if using salted butter)

1 tablespoon grated Parmesan or other grated hard cheese

Basil Garlic Butter

3 tablespoons butter

2 teaspoons puréed basil

1 clove garlic, put through press

Pinch of salt (omit if using salted butter)

1 tablespoon grated Parmesan or other grated hard cheese

Sage Garlic Butter

3 tablespoons butter

1 teaspoons minced fresh sage

1 clove garlic, put through press

Pinch of salt (omit if using salted butter)

1 tablespoon grated Parmesan or other grated hard cheese

Sweet-and-Spicy Sauce

Makes ½ cup

2 teaspoons hot Asian chili sauce

½ cup sweet chili sauce

Combine ingredients together and serve immediately.

VARIATIONS

Sweet-and-Hot Mustard Dip

Combine ½ cup sweet chili sauce or sweet relish with ½ cup Dijon mustard to make sweet-and-hot mustard dip.

Spicy Sweet Spread

Add 3 tablespoons sweet chili sauce to ½ cup mayonnaise to make a spicy sweet sandwich spread or salad dressing.

Spicy Sweet Dip

Add 1 teaspoon Asian chili sauce and 3 tablespoons sweet chili sauce to ½ cup plain yogurt or sour cream to make a dip.

Vinegar Dipping Sauce

Makes about 1 cup

1 cup cider vinegar

½ teaspoon pepper

½ teaspoon salt

½ teaspoon hot sauce

3 tablespoons brown sugar

1. Combine ingredients in small bowl. Mix thoroughly. Sauce will keep in covered container for several months.

2. Serve with ribs or other grilled meats.

Gypsy Gourmet

Spike this dipping sauce with 2 shots of your favorite spike, such as bourbon or dark rum.

Lime Butter

Enough for 2–3 pound flank steak

2 tablespoons butter

Juice of 2 limes, about 4 tablespoons

¼ teaspoon salt

1. Melt butter, then add lime juice and salt.

2. Serve warm with Cuban Marinated Flank Steak, Chapter 7.

Chipotle Dipping Sauce

Makes about ½ cup

½ cup mayonnaise

Juice of 2 limes, about 4 tablespoons

Pinch of salt

1 finely minced garlic clove or ½ teaspoon garlic powder

1½ teaspoons chipotle sauce

2 teaspoons sugar

1 tablespoon fresh cilantro, chopped (optional)

1. Whisk all ingredients together. Sauce can be stored for about a week in a covered container in the refrigerator.

2. Serve with Crab Cakes, Chapter 8, or grilled seafood or fish.

VARIATION

Chipotle Sour Cream Dipping Sauce

Substitute ½ cup sour cream or plain yogurt for the mayonnaise, then prepare as directed.

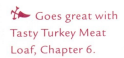 Goes great with Tasty Turkey Meat Loaf, Chapter 6.

White Gravy

Makes 1 cup

3 tablespoons butter

½ teaspoon salt

¼ teaspoon pepper

½ teaspoon garlic powder

⅛ teaspoon cayenne pepper or few dashes hot sauce, optional

½ cup cream or milk

3 tablespoons flour

½ cup chicken or vegetable stock

1. In a small sauce pan on medium heat, melt butter. Add salt, pepper, garlic powder, and hot sauce, if desired. Cook for 2–3 minutes.

2. Add milk, flour, and stock. Cook 2–3 minutes till bubbly, stirring till it turns to a smooth sauce.

Chipotle Orange BBQ Sauce

Makes 2 cups

2 tablespoons chipotle sauce

6 ounces frozen orange juice concentrate

6 garlic cloves, put through press

3 tablespoons sugar

1 6-ounce can tomato paste

1½ cups water

¼ teaspoon salt

1. In a small saucepan, combine the above ingredients and simmer 10–15 minutes till volume is reduced by half.

2. Serve with Tasty Turkey Meat Loaf, Chapter 6.

Gypsy Gourmet

To add a little more zing to the sauce, add:

- 1 tablespoon, plus 1 teaspoon molasses

- ½ teaspoon cumin powder

Honey Eggplant Hummus

Makes 3 cups and serves 6–8

Gypsy
Gourmet

For more authentic flavor, add 2 table-spoons tahini (sesame paste) to the mixture.

make your own tahini

To make your own tahini, toast 1 cup of sesame seeds in a 350°F oven for 3–4 minutes (keep an eye on them, they burn easily!). Put toasted sesame seeds in blender or food processer and add 1¼ tablespoons olive oil; blend into a paste. Cover and refrigerate. Can be kept for several weeks.

1 small eggplant (about ¾ pound)

3 cloves garlic, chopped

½ cup olive oil, divided into about 3 tablespoons and 5 tablespoons

Juice 1½ lemons, about 3 tablespoons

⅛ teaspoon salt

2–3 tablespoons honey

2 15.5-ounce cans of chick peas, rinsed

1. Preheat oven to 400°F.

2. Cover whole eggplant in foil and bake for 35 minutes until fork tender. Cool eggplant.

3. In a large food processor, mix garlic, 3 tablespoons of oil, lemon juice, and salt. Purée.

4. Cut off eggplant stem, then add in cooled whole eggplant and honey. Purée.

5. Add chick peas and remaining oil and blend until smooth. If the mixture is too thick, add in a tablespoon of water or oil. If you like it sweeter, add more honey.

6. Serve with pita chips and pita bread.

7. Keeps for about 4 to 5 days covered in refrigerator.

Wasabi Crème Sauce
for Seafood

Goes well with grilled fish.

Makes ½ cup

3 teaspoons wasabi powder

3 teaspoons water

⅛ teaspoon salt

6 tablespoons plain sour cream

1 teaspoon lemon juice

⅛ teaspoon garlic powder

1. In a small bowl, blend water and wasabi powder until a paste forms.

2. Whisk in remaining ingredients until sauce is blended. Will keep 1 week in refrigerator in a covered container.

Gorgonzola Cream Sauce

Makes ⅓ cup

¼ pound Gorgonzola Dolce or blue cheese of your choice

¼ cup cream

1. In small saucepan, heat gorgonzola and cream on low and mix till cheese is melted and sauce is well-blended.

2. Serve with Roasted Cauliflower with Gorgonzola Cream Sauce and Toasted Walnuts, Chapter 9.

Not-Quite-Homemade Salsa

Makes about 1 cup salsa

You can make not-quite-homemade green salsa by starting with a jar of green salsa.

1 7-ounce jar of salsa, any kind

2–3 tablespoons onion, chopped

Juice of 1 lime, about 2 tablespoons

¼ teaspoon salt

2 tablespoons fresh cilantro, chopped

2 tablespoons rice vinegar or cane vinegar, optional

Mix all ingredients together and serve.

Blue Cheese Dressing and Dip

Makes about 2 cups

¾ **cup plain sour cream**

1¼ **teaspoons salt**

½ **teaspoon pepper**

¾ **teaspoon garlic powder**

3 **tablespoons half-and-half or milk**

3 **tablespoons olive oil, preferably extra-virgin**

5 **tablespoons red onion, chopped**

1 **cup blue cheese, crumbled**

1. Mix together sour cream, salt, pepper, garlic powder, half-and-half, and olive oil till creamy.

2. For chunky dressing/dip, stir in onions and blue cheese. For creamy dressing, process all ingredients in a food processor until creamy.

3. Serve as a dressing for chopped salads or as a dip for chicken wings or vegetable crudités.

Gypsy Gourmet

Add 2 tablespoons red wine vinegar to the dip for extra zing.

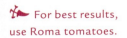

For best results, use Roma tomatoes.

Fresh Mexican Salsa

Makes about 1 cup

Gypsy Gourmet

Add 2 tablespoon rice vinegar or cane vinegar to the salsa for extra tang.

3–4 tomatoes (about 1 cup), seeded and chopped into small cubes.

Juice of 2 limes, about 4 tablespoons

1 tablespoon fresh cilantro, chopped

2–3 tablespoons red onion, chopped

½ teaspoon salt

1 small jalapeño, seeds removed and chopped fine

1. Combine all ingredients in a bowl. Serve with chips, in tacos or as a topping on grilled meats. This is best used the same day, so only make what you need.

VARIATION

Chipotle Sunshine Salsa

Add 1 teaspoon chipotle sauce, 1 teaspoon honey, ¼ teaspoon pepper, and the juice of 1 orange.

Fresh Tomatillo Salsa

Makes about 1½ cups

Use Serrano chilies for best results.

4–6 cloves garlic, minced

7–8 green tomatillos, husked and cored

1–2 whole chilies, depending on your preference for heat, tops cut off

2 tablespoons cooking oil

Juice of 1 lime, about 2 tablespoons

2 tablespoons onion, minced

2 tablespoons cilantro

¼ teaspoon salt

1 tablespoon rice vinegar or cane vinegar

1. In a medium nonstick pan over medium heat, sauté garlic, tomatillos, and chilies in the oil till slightly brown. Cool.

2. Add all ingredients to food processor and purée.

3. Will keep for 1 week in refrigerator.

4. Serve with grilled meat or use as a topping for Mexican dishes and eggs.

Red Chili Garlic Oil

Makes 1 cup

1 cup olive oil, preferably extra-virgin

2 teaspoons garlic, put through press

2 teaspoons crushed red chili flakes

½ teaspoon salt

1. In a 1-quart sauce pan on medium heat, add all ingredients and cook for 3–4 minutes.

2. Cool and serve with Paper Thin Tomato Basil Pizzas, Chapter 7 or Shrimp and Angel Hair Pasta, Chapter 8.

3. Keeps in refrigerator covered for up to 2 weeks. Warm in microwave 45–60 seconds each time before serving. Stir or shake for easy drizzling.

To use oil for bread dipping, add 2 tablespoons grated cheese (such as Parmesan) to ½ cup of warmed oil

Thyme Garlic Oil

Makes 1 cup

1 cup olive oil, preferably extra-virgin

2 teaspoons fresh thyme, stems off

2 teaspoons garlic, put through press

½ teaspoon salt

1. Heat olive oil in a small saucepan on medium heat.

2. Add thyme, garlic, and salt. Sauté for 3–4 minutes. Let cool.

3. Drizzle over Shrimp and Angel Hair Pasta, Chapter 8 or Paper Thin Tomato Basil Pizzas, Chapter 7. Also good with grilled vegetables and baked fish.

4. Store covered in refrigerator for up to 2 weeks. For easy drizzling, warm oil for 45–60 seconds on high in microwave when needed.

Red Sauce

Makes about two quarts

For extra zing to this recipe, add with the oregano and pepper:

- ¾ cup red wine (Cabernet or dry Italian red)
- ½ teaspoon crushed red pepper flakes
- ½ red pepper, minced

3 cups onions, chopped

3 tablespoons, plus 1 teaspoon garlic, put through press

¼ cup olive oil

2 28-ounce cans crushed tomatoes

1 6-ounce can tomato paste

1 cup chicken or vegetable stock (or substitute 1 cup water and 1 bouillon cube)

1 tablespoon oregano

1 teaspoon pepper

1 tablespoon sugar

½ teaspoon salt

3–4 bay leaves, whole

1 tablespoon whole fennel seeds (optional)

1 recipe Baked Turkey Meatballs, Chapter 6, if desired, or your favorite meatballs or sausage

8–10 basil leaves for garnish (optional)

1. In a large stock pot, sauté onions and garlic in olive oil on medium heat until onions turn transparent.

2. Add in tomatoes, paste, stock, oregano, pepper, sugar, salt, bay leaves, and fennel seeds (if using). Simmer 25–35 minutes.

3. Remove bay leaves and serve with your favorite pasta. If adding any meatballs or sausage to the sauce, add while simmering.

4. Garnish with 8–10 thinly sliced basil leaves just before serving, if desired.

extra layer of flavor To add an extra dimension of flavor to any hearty sauce, including this one: Sauté 2 tablespoons chopped pancetta in the olive oil first. Remove and discard the pancetta and add the onions and garlic to the drippings and olive oil. For an extra kick of garlic, reserve 1 teaspoon and add it just before serving.

Tartar Sauce

Makes about 1 cup

Gypsy
Gourmet

For a spicier kick, substitute 3 tablespoons sweet hot pepper relish for relish, or add ⅛ teaspoon cayenne pepper to the mix.

¾ cup mayonnaise

2 teaspoons garlic powder

2 tablespoons lemon juice

3 tablespoons relish

Pinch of salt

Blend all ingredients and serve with Baked Fish with Crispy Garlic Bread Crumbs, Chapter 8, or any fried or baked fish. Keeps for about 1 week covered in the refrigerator.

Garlic Vinaigrette

Makes about ½ cup

4 tablespoons olive oil, preferably extra-virgin

¾ teaspoon salt

2 tablespoons vinegar, preferably red wine vinegar

Juice of 1 lemon, about 2 tablespoons

½ teaspoon garlic, put through press

2 tablespoons water

In a small bowl, whisk together ingredients. Can keep covered in the refrigerator for 2–3 days. Serve over Red Leaf Lettuce Salad, Chapter 5.

Lemon Vinaigrette

Makes about ½ cup

¼ **cup olive oil, preferably extra-virgin**

1 clove garlic, put through press

2 tablespoons vinegar, preferably red wine vinegar

1 tablespoon water

¼ **teaspoon salt**

Juice of 1 lemon, about 2 tablespoons

In a small bowl, whisk together ingredients. Can be kept covered in refrigerator 2–3 days. Serve with lettuce salad, cold blanched green beans, or sliced cucumbers.

Lemon Shallot Vinaigrette

Makes about ¼ cup

¼ **cup olive oil, preferably extra-virgin**

Juice of 1 large lemon, about 2 tablespoons

¼ **teaspoon salt**

2 tablespoons shallots, minced fine

1 tablespoon, plus 2 teaspoons Dijon mustard

Whisk together in a small bowl. Can be kept covered in refrigerator 2–3 days. Serve with lettuce salad or grilled fish.

For best results, use Cortland apples and Bosc pears.

Cranberry, Pear, and Apple Chutney

Makes about 6 cups

Gypsy Gourmet

For a more special chutney, add to mixture:

- ½ cup cider vinegar
- ½ cup white raisins
- ½ cup port wine reduction sauce or ¼ cup good quality balsamic vinegar to which 1 tablespoon sugar and 2 tablespoons ruby port have been added.

3 cups apples, peeled and coarsely chopped

3 cups fresh cranberries, stems removed

3 cups pears, peeled and chopped

1½ cups light brown sugar, packed

1½ cups water

1¼ teaspoons fresh ginger, finely minced

1 teaspoon ground allspice

¾ teaspoon ground cloves

¼ teaspoon salt

1. Combine all ingredients in large pot. Cook over medium-high heat till mixture begins a gentle boil, stirring occasionally.

2. Reduce heat and simmer uncovered, stirring occasionally, until fruit is tender, around 30–35 minutes. Chutney should have a thick jam-like consistency and the fruit should be soft.

3. Cool and store in covered containers in the refrigerator for up to 4 months.

4. Serve with roast meats, chops, and cold chicken sandwiches.

Fresh Guacamole

Serves 6–8

6 ripe avocados, peeled and seeded

2 garlic cloves, put through a garlic press

1 tablespoon cilantro, minced

Juice of 2 limes, about 4 tablespoons

¼ teaspoon hot sauce

1 tablespoon red onion, finely minced

¼ teaspoon salt

2 tablespoons olive oil, preferably extra-virgin

1. Mash the above ingredients with a fork till blended. Let stand for 15 minutes before serving.

2. Serve with chips, or with your favorite Mexican dishes.

I use my own brand of hot sauce, Gypsy Juice, for this dip.

Gypsy Dip

Makes 1 cup

1 cup plain sour cream

5 tablespoons hot sauce

1. Mix together in small bowl.

2. Serve on baked potatoes, as a dip for vegetable crudités, nachos, or chicken wings, or use as a sandwich spread.

Lemon Garlic Sour Cream Sauce

Makes about 1 cup

8 ounces plain sour cream

Juice of 1 lemon, about 2 tablespoons

2 teaspoons garlic powder

½ teaspoon salt

1. Blend all ingredients well. Keeps covered in refrigerator up to 1 week.

2. Great dip for nachos, or served with any Mexican dish requiring a sour cream topping.

Caesar Salad Dressing

Makes about 1½ cups

2 large eggs (see Tip)

2 large garlic cloves, put through press

1 tablespoon mustard powder (I use Coleman's English, but regular Dijon works, too!)

¾ teaspoon salt

Juice of 1 lemon, about 2 tablespoons

1 teaspoon vinegar

½ teaspoon pepper

2 teaspoons Worcestershire sauce

1¼ cup oil, preferably sunflower, safflower, or light olive

1. Heat eggs in their shell in boiling water for 3 minutes.

2. In a food processor, combine all ingredients (except oil) and purée.

3. Drizzle small amounts of oil slowly into processor, blending till dressing becomes creamy.

4. Refrigerate dressing if not using immediately. Dressing will keep in refrigerator for about 3 days in a covered container. Dressing can be used as a marinade for pork, beef, or lamb.

Since raw eggs occasionally have bacteria contamination on them, this can be a concern with Caesar salad dressings and other condiments that use raw eggs as an ingredient. Adding the vinegar and cooking the eggs as instructed in this recipe helps kill bacteria and retard its growth. However, using pasteurized eggs or liquid egg products is encouraged to avoid this problem. Look for the USDA inspection mark on the egg container.

Gypsy Gourmet

For extra zing in the dressing, add 1 inch of anchovy paste from tube or 1 anchovy fillet.

Onion Chutney

Makes about 1½ cups

2 tablespoons olive oil

1½ tablespoons Asian chili sauce

2 teaspoons cumin (optional)

1 large onion, chopped (about 1–1½ cups)

1. Combine oil, chili sauce, and cumin (if desired). Blend to a paste. Add in onions, stir, and let mixture rest for ½ hour. Keeps in refrigerator for 2 days.

2. Perfect with grilled spiced meats, such as tandoori chicken, or Indian nan bread.

Spicy Peanut Dipping Sauce

Makes about 1 cup

⅓ cup peanut butter

½ teaspoon Asian chili sauce or hot sauce

1 cup water

1. Simmer ingredients in 2-quart saucepan on medium and stir till blended.

2. Use as a dip for fried foods, Vietnamese fresh rolls, or chicken and beef satay.

VARIATION

Ginger Peanut Dipping Sauce

Add 2 tablespoons fresh minced ginger while simmering.

Gypsy Gourmet

For extra zing, add 2 tablespoons hoisin sauce and/or 2 tablespoons rice vinegar before simmering.

Sweet Sauce

Makes ¾ cup

½ cup raisins, pitted prunes, or dried apricots

5 tablespoons hoisin sauce

¼ cup water

½ teaspoon grated ginger

1 clove garlic, put through press

1 teaspoon soy sauce

1. In a small saucepan on low heat, add together ingredients and simmer for 5–7 minutes. Cool.

2. Purée till smooth in food processor.

3. Serve with Vegetable Fried Rice, Chapter 9, and as a dipping sauce for egg rolls. Will keep covered in refrigerator for 1 week.

 VARIATION

Sweet Chutney with Nuts

While simmering, add 2 tablespoons minced onion and 2 tablespoons port or whiskey. A delicious option is to add 1 tablespoon chopped toasted walnuts to chutney after puréeing.

Dips, Spreads, and Sauces

Rosemary Applesauce

Serves 6

2 cups applesauce

1½ teaspoons powdered rosemary or 6" sprig fresh rosemary

2 tablespoons maple syrup or brown sugar

¼ teaspoon salt

1. Simmer ingredients in a quart saucepan on low for 7–8 minutes. Remove rosemary sprig. Can be eaten warm or at room temperature.

2. Serve with Garlic Roast Pork, Chapter 7.

Tuscan Bean Dip

Serves 4

Gypsy Gourmet

For extra flavor, add 1 tablespoon fresh thyme, taken off stem, and ½ teaspoon white wine vinegar to the mixture.

1 15-ounce can cannelloni beans, rinsed and drained

2 cloves garlic, put through press

3–4 tablespoons water

1 teaspoon salt

Juice of 1 large lemon, or 2 tablespoons lemon juice

¼ cup olive oil, a little more if you like your dip thinner

Dash of pepper

1. Process ingredients in food processor till creamy, then place in small bowl and let dip rest for 15 minutes.

2. Serve with pita chips, toasted baguettes, or use as a spread in roll-ups for grilled chicken and vegetables. Will keep in refrigerator 2–3 days.

Black Bean Dip

Makes about 1 cup

1 15.5-ounce can black beans, cooked, rinsed, and drained

½ teaspoon garlic powder

¼ teaspoon salt

2 tablespoons olive oil, preferably extra-virgin

2 tablespoons water

3–4 drops hot sauce, pinch of cayenne pepper, or few dashes Worcestershire sauce

1. Toss all ingredients in food processor or blender and purée.

2. May be served room temperature or warm. To warm, cook in microwave for 1½ minutes on high.

3. Serve with tortilla chips, or as a filling for burritos, or topping for nachos.

Crispy Garlic Croutons

Makes 4 cups

4 cups day-old bread, cut into small cubes (a baguette works best)

4 tablespoons butter

4 garlic cloves, put through press

¼ teaspoon pepper

¼ teaspoon salt

1. Preheat oven to 400°F.

2. In a large skillet on medium, melt butter. Sauté garlic till golden. Remove garlic.

3. Add in salt and pepper.

4. Toss in bread cubes and stir until all butter is absorbed.

5. Place on cookie sheet and bake till crispy, about 4–5 minutes, turning once.

6. These keep for about 1 week in a re-sealable bag.

CHAPTER 5

Soups and Salads

🚩 Cheeses that
work well for onion
soup and get stringy
when heated: Swiss,
mozzarella, Gruyère,
Emmental, or
Appenzeller.

Onion Soup with Cheese on the Bottom

Makes about 4 bowls

1 10-ounce can beef consommé or beef stock

1 14-ounce can chicken stock

2 tablespoons ketchup

2 bay leaves

2 cups water

½ teaspoon salt

3–4 sprigs thyme or 1 teaspoon dried thyme

2 tablespoons brandy or red wine, optional

4 cups onions, sliced thin

½ stick butter

1 tablespoon sugar

8–16 ounces your choice of cheese, divided into four servings

Gypsy Gourmet

You can deglaze the onion pan by ladling in some broth and scraping the pan, then adding broth back to soup. This gets all the yummy goodness from the onion pan and puts it in the soup!

1. In a 2-quart saucepan, on medium-high heat, bring stock, ketchup, bay leaves, water, salt, thyme, and brandy or wine (if desired) to a boil.

2. Reduce heat to medium and simmer.

3. In a 10" skillet on medium-high heat, sauté onions in the butter till tender, 5–8 minutes.

4. Add sugar and continue sautéing till onions start to just turn a bit brown. This process of caramelizing adds flavor to soup.

5. Add cooked onions to soup saucepan and simmer 10–15 minutes.

6. Remove bay leaves and thyme sprigs.

7. Place cheese in the bottom of four microwave-safe soup bowls and microwave on high 45 seconds to 1 minute, till melted.

8. Ladle in soup and serve.

VARIATION

Traditional French-Style Onion Soup

Place a piece of toasted bread at bottom of each bowl, cover with cheese and cook as directed above.

Lentil Sausage Soup

Serves 4

*Gypsy
Gourmet*

For a more flavorful soup, add ¼ cup chopped spinach.

1–2 links pork or chicken sausage, removed from casing or cut into small pieces

1 garlic clove, put through press

1 small onion, chopped

1 10-ounce can lentil soup

1 cup chicken stock

¾ cup water

¼ teaspoon oregano

Salt and pepper to taste

1. Heat a 2-quart saucepan on medium heat.

2. Add sausage and sauté 4–5 minutes (if out of casing, break up while sautéing).

3. Add garlic and onions and sauté 2–3 minutes.

4. Add soup, stock, water, and oregano and simmer 8–10 minutes. Salt and pepper to taste. Serve.

Black Bean Soup

Serves 6–8

1 pound dried black beans, cleaned

8 cups water

1 tablespoon garlic, put through press

3 bay leaves

2 teaspoons salt

¼ teaspoon pepper

3 cups onion, diced

1 vegetable bouillon cube (substitute beef or chicken)

1 recipe of Lemon Garlic Sour Cream, Chapter 4, and Fresh Mexican Salsa, Chapter 4

1. Place all ingredients in a large stockpot. Bring to a boil, then cover and reduce heat. Simmer on low for 1 hour and 20 minutes

2. Remove bay leaves before serving. Top with Lemon Garlic Sour Cream, Chapter 4, and Fresh Mexican Salsa, Chapter 4.

Gypsy
Gourmet

To spice this recipe up, add 2–3 dashes hot sauce, ½ teaspoon coriander, and 1½ tablespoons cumin.

Potato Soup with Garlic Croutons

Serves 4

Gypsy Gourmet

For more flavor, add in with the milk:

- Dash of hot cayenne powder
- ¼ teaspoon nutmeg

¾ cup chopped onion

3 tablespoons butter

2 14-ounce cans vegetable stock or chicken stock

½ cup water

½ teaspoon salt

¼ teaspoon pepper

2 bay leaves

3 cups potato, peeled, and chopped (Yukon Gold works best)

1 apple, peeled, cored, and chopped

1 cup milk (you may substitute half-and-half or more stock)

½ cup Crispy Garlic Croutons, Chapter 4, or your favorite kind

1. In a stockpot on medium heat, sauté onion in butter. Add in stock, water, salt, pepper, bay leaves, potato, and apple. Reduce heat and simmer for 20 minutes until potatoes are fork tender.

2. Remove bay leaves. If desired, purée while in pot with an immersion blender. Add in milk and simmer for 5 minutes on low. Serve with garlic croutons.

VARIATION

Kohlrabi-Potato Soup

Substitute 2 cups kohlrabi, peeled and cubed, for 2 cups potatoes.

Butternut Squash Soup

Serves 6–8

**2 large butternut squashes, about 4–5 pounds
(4 12-ounce packages frozen butternut squash or pumpkin
can be substituted)**

¾ stick butter

3 cups onion, minced

2 tablespoons garlic, put through press

6 cups chicken or vegetable stock

2 bay leaves

½ teaspoon salt

4 ounces plain sour cream

1 tablespoon fresh snipped chives

Crispy Garlic Croutons, Chapter 4, as many as desired

Gypsy Gourmet

For more dash, add
as the soup simmers:

- ¾ teaspoon
  nutmeg
- 2 tablespoons
  maple syrup or
  sugar
- 1 teaspoon of
  fresh minced
  ginger
- ¼ cup sherry

1. With a sharp knife poke 6–8 holes through each butternut squash. Place squash on microwave-safe dish and cook on high in microwave for 22–24 minutes till fork tender. Cool.

2. Cut squashes lengthwise and peel. Discard seeds.

3. In a large stock pot, melt butter and sauté onions and garlic till tender. Add squash, stock, bay leaves, and salt.

4. Simmer for 30–45 minutes (depending on your desired thickness—cooking longer makes the soup thicker).

5. Remove bay leaves. If desired, purée soup with hand-held immersion blender, then garnish with sour cream, chives, and croutons.

Nana's Corn Chowder

Makes 4–6 servings

🎀 Garnish with parsley, chopped scallion, and ground pepper.

¾ **stick unsalted butter**

1½ **cups onion, minced**

1 **garlic clove, put through press**

3 **ears of corn sliced off cob or 2 cups frozen or canned corn**

3½ **cups milk (for thicker chowder, substitute 1 cup half-and-half for 1 cup milk)**

¼ **teaspoon salt**

¼ **teaspoon pepper**

3 **bay leaves**

1 **vegetable bouillon cube (substitute beef or chicken)**

2 **tablespoons cornstarch or arrow root powder**

3 **tablespoons water**

1. In a stockpot, melt butter. Add onions, garlic, and corn and sauté for 2–3 minutes.

2. Add in milk, salt, pepper, bay leaves, and bouillon cube and simmer on low heat for 7–8 minutes.

3. In a small bowl, mix cornstarch or arrow root powder with water to form a paste with no lumps.

4. Add to soup, stirring as soup starts to thicken.

5. Remove bay leaves and serve.

Gypsy Gourmet

To add an extra layer of flavor to your chowder, follow these steps:

- Sauté 1 tablespoon chopped salt pork or pancetta till golden. Discard pork.

- Use drippings (plus butter) to sauté onions, garlic, and corn.

- Add 1½ tablespoons flat leaf parsley, chopped, and a few dashes of your favorite hot sauce as the chowder simmers.

- Add in 2 tablespoons sherry or 1 tablespoon sugar when you add in the cornstarch paste.

Zesty Zucchini Soup

Serves 4–6

2 cups zucchini, sliced

3 tablespoons onion, chopped

2–3 garlic cloves, put through press

2 tablespoons olive oil, preferably extra-virgin

3 cups chicken or vegetable stock

½ teaspoon salt

¼ teaspoon pepper

½ cup cream or half-and-half (in a pinch, milk may be substituted)

2 tablespoons lemon juice

2 tablespoons chives, snipped

½ cup plain sour cream

¼ cup Crispy Garlic Croutons, Chapter 4

1. In a stockpot on medium heat, sauté zucchini, onion, and garlic in olive oil till tender.

2. Add in stock, salt, and pepper and simmer for 20–25 minutes.

3. Add in cream and simmer 4–5 minutes.

4. If desired, purée with immersion blender.

5. Just before serving, add lemon juice.

6. Ladle into bowls and top each bowl with chives, plain sour cream, and Crispy Garlic Croutons, Chapter 4.

Gypsy Gourmet

To give the soup more body, add 8 ounces of plain yogurt. For more flavor, add in 1 cup fresh basil leaves and a few dashes hot sauce while simmering, then add 1 tablespoon fresh tarragon, minced, just before serving.

Simple Tomato-Orange Soup

Serves 2

1 10-ounce can tomato or tomato bisque soup

Juice of 1 large orange or ¼ cup orange juice

1 cup chicken stock

½ cup cream, half-and-half, or milk

In a 2-quart stockpot, mix together ingredients and cook on medium-low heat for 5–7 minutes.

VARIATIONS

Tomato-Orange Dill Soup

Add ½ teaspoon dry dill to above recipe.

Chipotle-Orange Tomato Soup

Add ⅛ teaspoon chipotle sauce and ¼ teaspoon garlic powder to above recipe.

Shrimp and Corn Tomato soup

Add 6 medium shrimp, cooked, and 2–3 tablespoons corn to the recipe.

Gypsy Gourmet

To add extra zing to the soup, replace the orange juice with 2 teaspoons of Triple Sec or Cointreau liqueur and the zest of 1 orange. Garnish with:

- Plain yogurt or sour cream
- Bacon bits
- Fresh-snipped chives
- Herb or Garlic Croutons, Chapter 4

Cream of Mushroom Soup

Serves 2

1 10-ounce can cream of mushroom soup

1 cup chicken or vegetable stock

½ cup cream, half-and-half, or milk

¼ teaspoon garlic powder

In a 2-quart stockpot, mix together ingredients and cook on medium-low heat for 5–7 minutes.

Gypsy Gourmet

To add extra zing to the soup, add 1 tablespoon sherry or sweet Marsala wine and garnish with croutons and freshly snipped chives.

Red Leaf Lettuce Salad with Vinaigrette

Gypsy Gourmet

Make it creamy by adding ¼ cup cream and omitting the cucumbers.

Serves 4–6

2 large heads red leaf lettuce, washed

2 small tomatoes, seeded and cut into cubes or wedges

2 cucumbers, peeled and diced

1 medium red onion, peeled and cut into thin rings

¾ cup croutons

1 recipe Garlic Vinaigrette, Chapter 4, or Lemon Shallot Vinaigrette, Chapter 4

1. Remove outer leaves of lettuce and core. Discard. Chop remaining lettuce and place in large salad bowl.

2. Add tomatoes, cucumbers, and onion. Top with croutons and vinaigrette.

Avocado-Grape Tomato Salad with Lemon Vinaigrette

Serves 4

3–4 ripe avocados, pit removed, peeled, and chopped

1 medium red onion, chopped into slivers

2 cups grape tomatoes, cut into halves

1 recipe Lemon Vinaigrette, Chapter 4

1. In a large bowl, add avocado, onion, and tomatoes.

2. Toss with Lemon Vinaigrette and serve.

🚩 To add color and texture to coleslaw, add ¼ cup of shredded red cabbage and/or 1 shredded carrot.

Apple-Jalapeño Coleslaw

Serves 6–8

1 medium head cabbage, shredded (5–6 cups)

2 apples, preferably Granny Smith

½ cup cider vinegar

¼ cup oil

1½ teaspoons salt

1 medium jalapeño, stem removed, or a few dashes of hot sauce

¼ cup sugar

½ teaspoon cinnamon

1 teaspoon pepper

1. In a large bowl, shred the cabbage (it should yield 5–6 cups). Then core and cut the apples into matchstick slices or cubes and add to bowl.

2. Purée the vinegar, oil, salt, jalapeño, sugar, cinnamon, and pepper in a blender. Add to cabbage-and-apple mixture. Chill and serve.

Gypsy Gourmet

For a little more kick in the dressing, add:

- ½ teaspoon powdered clove
- 2 tablespoons horseradish
- ¼ cup raisins or golden raisins
- ¼ cup chopped nuts, such as walnut or pecan

Lentil-Eggplant Salad

Serves 6–8

1 medium eggplant

½ teaspoon salt

4 tablespoons olive oil (preferably extra-virgin), divided

1 small onion chopped, preferably red onion

2 cloves garlic, put through press

1 tablespoon vinegar

Juice of 1 lemon, about 2 tablespoons

Fresh ground pepper

1 12–15-ounce can lentils, rinsed and drained, or cook 1 cup from scratch

1. Preheat oven to 350°F.

2. Trim off top of eggplant and cut into cubes. Place eggplant on nonstick baking sheet. Season with salt and drizzle 2 tablespoons oil over eggplant. Toss.

3. Bake for 12–15 minutes, turning once. Cool.

4. In a large bowl, add onion, garlic, vinegar, lemon, remainder of olive oil, and pepper. Mix together.

5. Add lentils and eggplant. Serve.

Gypsy Gourmet

To give this extra appeal, add 1 cup cooked faro (wheat berries) and 2 tablespoons flat leaf parsley at the end, with the eggplant.

Feta and Carrot Salad

Serves 6–8

2 bunches carrots, peeled and chopped

¼ cup olive oil, preferably extra-virgin

Juice of 1 lemon, about 2 tablespoons

1 tablespoon oregano

1 teaspoon garlic powder

1 tablespoon fresh snipped chives, optional

2–3 tablespoons crumbled feta cheese

1. In a large saucepan or stock pot, boil 4 cups salted water on medium-high. Add carrots. Cook till almost fork tender.

2. Rinse carrots in cool water and let cool.

3. In a large bowl, mix oil, lemon, oregano, garlic, and chives (if desired). Add in carrots and toss. Add cheese and toss.

4. Chill for 30 minutes, then serve.

Soups and Salads

Caesar Salad

Serves 4

1 head romaine lettuce, cleaned, and chopped

1 recipe Caesar Salad Dressing, Chapter 4

½ cup Crispy Garlic Croutons, Chapter 4, or your favorite croutons

3–4 tablespoons grated Parmesan cheese

Pepper to taste

1. In a large salad bowl, combine lettuce with ¾ cup dressing. Add croutons and toss.

2. Plate salad and sprinkle generous amounts of cheese on each. Serve with fresh ground pepper.

Chickpea Cucumber Salad

Serves 4–6

Gypsy Gourmet

To spice this dish up a little, add 3 tablespoons chopped parsley and ⅓ cup Greek or black olives.

1 15.5-ounce can of chick peas, rinsed and drained

¼ cup olive oil, preferably extra-virgin

3 tablespoons onion, sliced thin (preferably red for color and taste!)

½ teaspoon salt

Juice of ½ lemon, about 1 tablespoon

1 carrot, peeled and shredded

1 cucumber, peeled and thinly sliced

1 tablespoon vinegar

2 garlic cloves, put through press

¼ teaspoon pepper

Combine all ingredients in a medium salad bowl. Toss and serve.

Collard Greens Salad

Serves 6–8

¼ cup olive oil

¼ teaspoon pepper

1 teaspoon salt

1 tablespoon water

Juice of one lemon, optional

2 tablespoons vinegar

3 garlic cloves, put through press

4–5 cups fresh collard greens, washed and cut thin (remove stems)

1–2 tomatoes, seeded and diced into small cubes

1 medium onion, thinly sliced

1. In a small bowl, whisk together oil, pepper, salt, water, lemon (if desired), vinegar, and garlic. Set aside dressing.

2. In a large bowl, combine greens, onion, and tomatoes. Toss with dressing.

3. Let salad rest for 30 minutes, tossing a few times as it rests. Serve.

Gypsy Gourmet

For extra flavor, add 1 15-ounce can of rinsed and drained beans, such as red kidney or black beans.

Greek Salad

Serves 4

2 tablespoons vinegar

½ teaspoon salt

2 tablespoons water

3–4 tablespoons olive oil, preferably extra-virgin

1 head iceberg lettuce chopped (or substitute green leaf)

1 small onion, sliced fine

¼ cup Greek olives

1 tomato, seeded and chopped

1 cucumber, peeled and cubed

1 small pepper, red or green, seeded and cubed

½ cup feta cheese, crumbled

1. Whisk together vinegar, salt, water, and olive oil and set dressing aside.

2. In a large salad bowl, combine remaining ingredients. Toss with dressing.

3. Serve with warm pita bread.

Poultry Dishes

If you prefer, you can skip the nuts and use 2 cups cooked, peeled, and mashed Japanese yams. These have the texture, body and many of the same flavors of roasted chestnuts.

Roasted Chicken with Nut Stuffing

Serves 4–6

1 whole chicken (about 4–6 pounds), roasted

6 slices bread

1 stick butter

1½ cups onion, chopped

1 teaspoon garlic powder

½ teaspoon salt

¼ teaspoon pepper

1 cup bread crumbs

½ cup chopped nuts of your choice: walnuts, pecans, almonds, or 2 cups chestnuts (if using chestnuts, use the unsweetened jarred or canned variety, or cook, peel, and coarsely chop fresh chestnuts)

¾ cup chicken stock

Gypsy Gourmet

To make this stuffing extra-special, add:

- ½ cup golden raisins
- ¼ cup dry Marsala wine

1. Purchase roasted chicken from grocery, or prepare uncooked chicken to your taste. Keep warm in a 200°F oven.

2. Cut bread into cubes, including crust, and set aside.

3. In a saucepan on medium, melt butter, then add onions and sauté till tender. Add bread cubes, garlic powder, salt, pepper, bread crumbs, and nuts. Mix together. Add chicken stock and toss till moistened.

4. Transfer stuffing to 9" × 13" baking dish. Remove chicken from oven and let rest. Increase oven temperature to 350°F and bake stuffing for 15 minutes, or until lightly browned.

Garlic Stuffed Roasted Chicken

Serves 3–4

1 whole chicken (3–4 pounds), rinsed and patted dry

½ stick softened butter

Salt and pepper to taste

2–3 whole heads garlic (not cloves), skins on

1. Preheat oven to 375°F.

2. Rub butter all over chicken. Season with salt and pepper, inside and out. Stuff neck cavity with garlic bulbs till full.

3. Roast 1 hour and 15 minutes. Rest bird in oven 10 minutes with heat off.

4. Place on platter and serve with favorite sides.

If you love garlic, remove heads from cavity and serve garlic on a plate, or squeeze cloves onto warm crusty bread.

Gypsy Gourmet

For a more fragrant, flavorful meal, place thyme inside bottom cavity when stuffing chicken. Two rosemary sprigs can be used in place of thyme, or substitute 1 teaspoon of crushed rosemary leaves, if you prefer.

Baked Turkey Meatballs

Makes 10–12 turkey balls

1 pound ground turkey

1 teaspoon salt

1½ teaspoons oregano

¼ teaspoon pepper

1 tablespoon garlic powder

½ cup bread crumbs

1 egg

1 tablespoon olive oil

2 tablespoons cornstarch

4 tablespoons flat leaf parsley, chopped (optional)

½ cup onion

¼ cup Romano cheese, grated

1 recipe Red Sauce, Chapter 4

1. Preheat oven to 425°F. Line a cookie sheet with foil and grease the foil.

2. Combine ingredients, mixing well, then shape into balls. Place on cookie sheet about an inch apart. Bake 20–22 minutes, turning once.

3. Serve with Red Sauce, Chapter 4.

Southwestern Chicken

Rub can be saved in air tight container or baggie up to 2 months.

Makes about ½ cup, or enough to coat 3–4 pounds meat

1 tablespoon chili powder

1 teaspoon cumin

¼ teaspoon salt

⅛ teaspoon cayenne pepper

1 teaspoon garlic powder

1 tablespoon brown sugar

2–3 pounds boneless skinless chicken breasts

2 tablespoons oil

1. Combine chili powder, cumin, salt, pepper, garlic powder, and sugar in a small bowl. Mix thoroughly and set aside.

2. Coat chicken breasts with oil, then sprinkle on rub and let chicken sit for 15 minutes.

3. Preheat oven to 375°F.

4. Bake chicken on greased baking sheets for 25–35 minutes, till juices run clear.

Chicken Cutlets with Red Sauce

Serves 4

Gypsy Gourmet

Veal can be substituted for chicken. For extra flavor, add 2 tablespoons grated Parmesan cheese to the bread crumb mixture before breading cutlets.

2–3 pounds boneless, skinless chicken breasts, rinsed and dried

½ cup all-purpose flour

¼ cup water

2 large eggs

1½ cups bread crumbs

1½ tablespoons oregano

½ teaspoon salt

¼ teaspoon pepper

2 teaspoons garlic powder

2½–3 cups cooking oil

1 pound mozzarella cheese slices or 2–3 cups grated mozzarella

1 recipe Red Sauce, Chapter 4

1. Slice chicken breasts through center in half, then pound halves into thin cutlets, trimming away any irregular pieces. Set aside.

2. Place flour in medium bowl and set aside.

3. In a medium bowl, whisk together the water and eggs, then set aside.

4. In a medium bowl or bag, combine bread crumbs, oregano, salt, pepper, and garlic powder. Set aside.

5. Coat chicken with flour, then dip in egg wash, and, finally, dredge through bread crumb mix, making sure both sides are covered.

6. In a 10" skillet, add oil to one-third full. Heat on medium-high. Oil is ready when drop of batter added sizzles.

7. Fry 2–3 cutlets at a time for 3–4 minutes on each side. Cutlets are done when crumbs turn golden brown.

8. Transfer to a cooling rack placed over a baking sheet.

9. Set oven to broil.

10. Place a handful of grated or a few slices of mozzarella cheese over each cutlet, then place under broiler for 1½–2 minutes till melted. Transfer to individual plates.

11. Ladle plate with Red Sauce, Chapter 4, and top with 1–2 cutlets.

Chicken Salad

Makes about 4–5 pounds

Gypsy Gourmet

For something special, add in any combination of the following to the mayonnaise mixture:

- 3 tablespoons flat leaf parsley, minced

- 1 tablespoon red wine vinegar or regular vinegar

- 3 tablespoons sugar

- 2 tablespoons olive oil, preferably extra-virgin

- 1½ teaspoons paprika

- 1 tablespoon Dijon mustard

- 2 tablespoons fresh tarragon, minced

- 2–3 dashes hot sauce

- ¾ cup chopped walnuts

- ¾ cup dried cranberries or raisins

4–5 pounds skinless boneless chicken breasts, cooked

1¼–1½ cups mayonnaise

4 tablespoons red onion, chopped, or 3 scallions, white and green parts sliced thin (or use both if you like!)

3 celery stalks, chopped

1 teaspoon salt

½ teaspoon pepper

3 tablespoons lemon juice

2 teaspoons garlic powder

1. Cut breasts into desired size cubes and set aside.

2. In a large bowl, mix together mayonnaise, onion, celery, salt, pepper, lemon juice, and garlic powder.

3. Add in cubed chicken and stir until coated. Serve.

Crispy Battered Fried Chicken

Serves 4

1 cup all-purpose flour

1½ teaspoons pepper

1 teaspoon salt

2½–3 cups cooking oil

3–5 pounds chicken drums and thighs, with skin

Hot sauce to taste

1. In a gallon re-sealable plastic bag, add flour, pepper, and salt. Shake to mix.

2. Place one piece of chicken at a time in the batter bag and shake until coated. Set aside until all chicken is coated.

3. Add cooking oil to 12" skillet to about one-third full. Heat on medium-high until a drop of batter added to the oil sizzles. Add chicken to the hot oil in batches of 3–4. Don't crowd the pan by adding too much chicken at once.

4. Turn every 3–4 minutes till skin turns golden, for about 15 minutes per batch.

5. Serve with favorite hot sauce and sides.

You can also make crispy battered fried turkey using this recipe. Do 2 drums or thighs at a time. It takes 25–35 minutes cooking time.

Gypsy Gourmet

Add 4 tablespoons blackening seasoning to the flour coating for extra zing. To make chicken extra-tender and tasty, brine it ahead of time by placing 5–6 cups of water and ½ teaspoon salt in a re-sealable plastic bag. Add chicken pieces. Let marinate for at least 6 hours (and up to 36 hours) in the refrigerator before frying.

You can also use 2 whole chickens instead of chicken parts. Marinate as directed, then roast in oven at 375°F for about 90 minutes, till juices run clear.

Cuban Chicken

Serves 4–6

¾ cup vinegar, preferably cane or cider vinegar

3 tablespoons garlic, put through garlic press

3 tablespoons sugar

3 tablespoons olive oil, preferably extra-virgin

¾ cup onion, chopped

1 tablespoon salt

1 teaspoon pepper

4–6 pounds chicken parts

Gypsy Gourmet

For more flavor, add to the marinade: 3 tablespoons cumin and 2 tablespoons achiote powder.

1. Combine all ingredients (except chicken) in re-sealable bag and mix. Then add chicken.

2. Marinate in refrigerator overnight and up to 2 days for best results, turning bag occasionally.

3. Preheat oven to 375°F. Place foil on 2 cookie sheets; oil the foil. Put chicken on prepared cookie sheets, not letting pieces touch.

4. Cook 45 minutes to 1 hour, until done.

Strawberry Honey Mustard Crumb Chicken Breast

Serves 4

¼ cup strawberry fruit spread or jam

1½ teaspoons soy sauce

3 tablespoons honey mustard

½ teaspoon garlic powder

2–4 pounds boneless skinless chicken breasts

¾ cup bread crumbs

3 tablespoons butter, melted

1. Preheat oven to 400°F.

2. Place a sheet of foil on a cookie sheet and lightly grease the foil.

3. In a shallow dish, mix together the strawberry fruit spread, soy sauce, honey mustard, and garlic powder.

4. Dip chicken breasts in strawberry glaze and place on prepared cookie sheet.

5. Mix together bread crumbs and melted butter. Top chicken breasts with crumb topping.

6. Bake 20–25 minutes. Serve.

Gypsy Gourmet

If you find regular bread crumbs turn out too dry, try panko crumbs! For a special variation, purée 2 tablespoons of slivered almonds and add them to the bread crumb topping.

Chicken with Green Beans and Pineapple

Serves 4–6

3–4 pounds chicken parts (any parts)

2 tablespoons cooking oil

4 cups onions, chopped

3 tablespoons garlic, put through press

¼ cup rice vinegar

1 13.5-ounce can unsweetened coconut milk

1 10-ounce can pineapple chunks in own juice, separated

½ cup curry powder

2 tablespoons ginger, grated

½ cup water

1 vegetable bouillon cube (substitute beef or chicken)

3 bay leaves

¼ teaspoon pepper

10 ounces canned or frozen green beans

1. In a large skillet set on high, brown chicken parts in oil. Add onions and garlic. Reduce heat and sauté. Add vinegar, coconut milk, and pineapple juice, reserving pineapple chunks. Add curry powder, ginger, water, bouillon, bay leaves, and pepper. Cover and cook on low simmer for 45 minutes. Add pineapple chunks and green beans.

2. Cook on low heat, uncovered, for another 10–15 minutes until sauce is like a gravy. Remove bay leaves. Serve over rice.

Grilled Jerk Chicken with Pineapple and Peppers

Serves 4–6

1 20-ounce can pineapple chunks in pineapple juice

2½ tablespoons jerk seasoning

1 tablespoon garlic, put through press

1 tablespoon cooking oil

3–4 pounds boneless, skinless chicken breasts, cut into large cubes

1–2 large onions, peeled and quartered

1 each red, yellow, and green peppers cored and cut into cubes (optional)

Gypsy Gourmet

Fresh ripe pineapple can be used in place of canned. Just add 12 ounces of real pineapple juice when making marinade.

1. Open can of pineapple chunks and pour juice into a large re-sealable plastic bag. Reserve pineapple chunks.

2. Add jerk seasoning, garlic, and oil to pineapple juice. Mix together.

3. Add chicken and marinate at least 30 minutes in the refrigerator. (Can also be marinated overnight.)

4. Heat grill on high for 10 minutes.

5. On skewers, layer onion, chicken, pineapple cubes, and peppers (if desired). Baste with remaining marinade.

6. Sear skewers on both sides, then reduce heat to medium.

7. Cook 7–10 minutes on each side with lid down.

🐦 Chicken can be baked in oven on lightly greased, foil-lined cookie sheets at 375°F for 45 minutes or until cooked through.

Grilled Lemon Herb Chicken Breasts

Serves 4–6

6 cloves garlic, minced

1 tablespoon honey

Juice of 2 lemons, 4 tablespoons

3 tablespoons olive oil

1 teaspoon salt

1 tablespoon Dijon mustard

1 teaspoon pepper

1 tablespoon fresh thyme (leaves off stem)

3–4 pounds boneless, skinless chicken breasts

1. Combine all ingredients (except chicken) in a large re-sealable plastic bag. Mix together. Add chicken and marinate at least 1 hour (overnight for best results).

2. Grill chicken breasts on medium heat till done.

Gypsy Gourmet

To spice up the marinade, add:

- 2 teaspoons white wine vinegar
- Zest from 1 lemon
- 2–3 dashes hot sauce
- 2 minced shallots
- ¼ cup white wine or dry vermouth
- ¼ teaspoon paprika

Chicken Burritos with Caramelized Onions

Serves 4

8 6" soft flour tortillas

2 tablespoons oil

2 medium onions, sliced thin

2 large chicken breasts, trimmed and cut into thin strips

4 cloves garlic, put through press

½ cup chicken stock

¼ teaspoon salt

4 tablespoons ketchup

Few drops hot sauce

Shredded lettuce or chopped tomatoes (optional)

1 recipe of Lemon Garlic Sour Cream, Chapter 4; Chipotle Dipping Sauce, Chapter 4; Fresh Mexican Salsa, Chapter 4; or Black Bean Dip, Chapter 4

1. Wrap tortillas in foil and warm in 300°F oven for 10 minutes.

2. Heat oil in a 12" skillet on medium heat. Fry onions till they just start to turn golden. Drain and remove onions and set them aside.

3. Turn skillet to medium-high heat. Fry chicken in oil 3–4 minutes, turning once. Add garlic, stock, salt, ketchup, and hot sauce. Cook till no liquid remains in pan. Return onions to pan and toss while cooking, 1–2 minutes.

4. Fill warmed tortilla with filling and add lettuce or tomatoes, if desired.

Gypsy Gourmet

To spice up the meat mixture, add:

- 1 tablespoon cumin

- 1 teaspoon chili powder

- ½ teaspoon ground coriander

- Pinch of cayenne

- Top with your choice of Lemon Garlic Sour Cream, Chapter 4; Chipotle Dipping Sauce, Chapter 4, Fresh Mexican Salsa, Chapter 4; or Black Bean Dip, Chapter 4

Crust Dust for Chicken Legs

Serves 4

4 large chicken legs, washed and patted dry

2 tablespoons cooking oil

1 tablespoon, plus 1 teaspoon garlic powder

2 teaspoons paprika

¾ teaspoon salt

½ teaspoon pepper

1 tablespoon, plus 1 teaspoon flour

1. Preheat oven to 375°F. Grease lipped cookie sheet.

2. Place chicken legs on sheet and rub top of chicken with oil.

3. In a small bowl, mix together remaining ingredients.

4. Coat chicken with mixture ("crust dust").

5. Bake 55 minutes to 1 hour, turning occasionally to so chicken cooks evenly.

6. Serve with Collard Greens, Chapter 5, Confetti Macaroni and Cheese, Chapter 9, corn on cob, and/or potatoes.

Turkey Tacos

Serves 4–6

1 pound ground turkey (or 1 pound ground meat of your choice)

2 tablespoons cooking oil

1 onion, minced

3 cloves garlic, put through press

5 tablespoons ketchup

½ cup chicken stock

Pinch of salt

2–3 dashes hot sauce

12 white or yellow taco shells, warmed per shell manufacturer's instruction

Your choice fillings (see list)

In a 12" skillet on medium, brown turkey in oil with onions and garlic. Add ketchup, stock, salt, and hot sauce. Cook till light sauce is formed and no liquid remains. Fill taco shells and serve with your choice of fillings.

To add a delicious flavor to the meat mixture, add while cooking:

- 1 tablespoon cumin

- 2 teaspoons chili powder

- Pinch of cayenne pepper

fillings for tacos

Use any or all of these as fillings for the tacos:

- 1½ cups Fresh Mexican Salsa, Chapter 4, or your favorite

- 1 cup plain sour cream

- ½ cup chopped tomatoes

- 1 cup shredded lettuce

- ½ cup chopped onions

- ¾ cup guacamole

- 2 thin sliced scallions

- ¼ cup jalapeños, minced

Mediterranean Chicken

Serves 4–6

2–3 pounds chicken thighs and drum sticks, skin on

4 tablespoons olive oil, divided

3 cups onion, chopped

4 bay leaves

½ teaspoon salt

¼ teaspoon pepper

2–3 dashes hot sauce

1 28-ounce can crushed tomatoes

1 6-ounce can tomato paste

1 teaspoon fresh rosemary, minced fine

1 teaspoon oregano

¾ teaspoon paprika

1 cup chicken stock

Juice and zest of 2 lemons (about 4 tablespoons juice)

1 teaspoon garlic, minced

6–8 basil leaves, chopped (optional)

3–4 tablespoons grated Parmesan cheese

1. Heat 2 tablespoons olive oil in a large skillet. Add chicken and brown on both sides. Set aside.

2. Discard drippings, reserving about 2 tablespoons of olive oil in skillet.

3. Sauté onions in pan drippings until tender. Return chicken to pan.

4. Add bay leaves, salt, pepper, and hot sauce. Simmer on medium 4–5 minutes

5. Add tomatoes, tomato paste, rosemary, oregano, paprika, and stock. Cover and simmer for 20 minutes.

6. Stir in lemon juice and zest, garlic, and basil (if desired). Turn chicken pieces.

7. Simmer 7–10 minutes. Sauce will be slightly thick. Remove bay leaves.

8. Plate. Drizzle with remaining olive oil and top with grated Parmesan.

Gypsy Gourmet

For more intense flavor, after sautéing the onion, add:

- ¼ cup dry white wine or dry vermouth
- ½ red pepper (chopped)
- 2 tablespoons minced garlic
- For more Mediterranean flavor, add ¼ cup pitted and halved Kalamata olives with the tomatoes

Vietnamese Spicy Ground Meat Salad with Peanuts

Serves 2–4

½ pound ground chicken or turkey

2–3 cloves garlic, put through a press

1 tablespoon cooking oil

1 tablespoon peanut oil

3 tablespoons rice vinegar

Juice of 1 lime, about 2 tablespoons

1 teaspoon fish sauce or soy sauce

1 head lettuce, shredded fine

¼ cup dry-roasted unsalted peanuts, chopped fine

1. In a 10" skillet, brown meat and garlic in cooking oil. Break up meat while cooking. When done, let cool.

2. In a small bowl, make dressing by mixing together peanut oil, vinegar, lime juice, and fish sauce or soy sauce. Set aside.

3. Place shredded lettuce on plates. Add meat mixture, top with toasted chopped peanuts, then drizzle with dressing just before serving.

Gypsy Gourmet

To add more kick to the meat mixture, add 1 teaspoon dry red chili flakes and ¼ cup chicken or vegetable stock during the browning stage, simmering until liquid is absorbed. For a fresh Vietnamese taste, garnish with:

- 1½ tablespoons peeled fresh ginger, cut into thin julienne strips

- 2 tablespoons fresh cilantro leaves, separated

- 1 small sliced red onion, about ½ cup

Tandoori Chicken

Serves 4

¾ cup plain yogurt

1 tablespoon garlic, put through press

2 tablespoons paprika

1½ teaspoons cumin

1 teaspoon salt

4–6 large skinless chicken legs

2 lemons, cut for squeezing (optional)

1. In a bowl combine yogurt with all spices and mix.

2. Put chicken in a large re-sealable bag and cover with Tandoori seasoning. Marinate 6 hours.

3. Preheat oven to 400°F.

4. Remove chicken from bag and place chicken on lightly greased, foil-lined baking sheets. Cook for 45 minutes.

5. Squeeze lemons over top, if desired.

6. Serve with rice and Onion Chutney, Chapter 4.

Gypsy Gourmet

For more authentic Indian flavor, add to the marinade:

- 1 tablespoon, plus 1 teaspoon ground coriander

- ⅛ teaspoon cayenne pepper

- 1 tablespoon ginger, grated

- ½ teaspoon cardamom

Tasty Turkey Meat Loaf

Serves 4–6

Meat mixture can be shaped into patties and cooked as turkey burgers.

2 pounds ground turkey

¾ cup onion, minced

1½ teaspoons salt

1 tablespoon garlic powder

1½ teaspoons pepper

¾ cup bread crumbs

2 tablespoons poultry seasoning, optional

3 tablespoons cornstarch, if needed

1 egg

¼ cup unsweetened applesauce

1 recipe White Gravy, Chapter 4, or Chipotle Orange BBQ Sauce, Chapter 4

1. Preheat oven to 375°F.

2. Mix all ingredients together well. If using extra-lean ground turkey (85 percent or less), add in cornstarch to help make mixture adhere.

3. Form meat mixture into 2 loaves and place into greased loaf pans. Cook 40–45 minutes.

4. Serve with White Gravy, Chapter 4, or Chipotle Orange BBQ Sauce, Chapter 4.

Gypsy Gourmet

For an extra spicy meatloaf, add to the meat mixture:

- 1–2 dashes hot sauce

- 2 tablespoons olive oil, preferably extra-virgin

- 1 red jalapeño, seeded and chopped fine

- 1 green jalapeño, seeded, chopped fine

CHAPTER 7

Beef and Other Meats

Garlic Roast Pork with Rosemary Applesauce

Serves 4–12, depending on roast size
(plan ½ pound per serving)

2 tablespoons cooking oil

2 teaspoons garlic powder or 3 garlic cloves, put through a press

2 tablespoons, plus 2 teaspoons soy sauce

2–6 pound center-cut roast or loin roast of pork

1 recipe Rosemary Applesauce, Chapter 4

1. Preheat oven to 350°F.

2. In a small bowl, whisk together oil, garlic, and soy sauce. Coat entire roast with mixture.

3. Bake in roasting pan to desired doneness, about 16–18 minutes a pound for medium done pork (pink in center). Allow 15 minutes for pork to rest before serving.

4. Serve with Rosemary Applesauce, Chapter 4.

🪓 Sauce can also be used on pork ribs or chops.

Grilled Ham Steaks with Cinnamon City BBQ Sauce

Serves 6–8 (allow about ½ pound per serving)

Gypsy Gourmet

To add zing to this meal, add:

- 2–3 hot or mild sliced cherry peppers, minced, more if you like hot
- 1 cup BBQ sauce

1 cup ketchup

1 tablespoon cinnamon

¼ cup cider vinegar

¼ cup packed brown sugar or corn syrup

2 teaspoons garlic powder

¼ teaspoon hot sauce or cayenne pepper, optional

4–6 large ham steaks (3–4 pounds)

1. In a medium-size bowl, mix all ingredients together (except ham).

2. Grill ham steaks over high heat, 2-3 minutes per side. Reduce heat to medium or low, and brush sauce on ham steaks. Finish cooking another 5-7 minutes and serve.

Corned Beef Hash Mash

Serves 4–6

¾ **stick butter**

2 large potatoes, peeled, cooked, and mashed

1 teaspoon garlic powder

1 12-ounce can corned beef hash or 12-ounce chopped cooked corn beef

1 large onion, minced (2 cups)

Salt and pepper to taste

1. Heat a 10" skillet on medium heat and melt butter.

2. Add potatoes and garlic powder. Break up potatoes while frying. Fry till golden and crispy brown. Remove from pan. Set aside.

3. In same skillet, turn heat to high. Fry corned beef. Break apart meat while cooking. Fry till meat starts to turn crispy brown.

4. Add onions to hash. Reduce heat to medium-high. Cook till onions are tender.

5. Return potatoes to pan and fry till meat and potatoes are crispy.

6. Season with salt and pepper and serve.

After cooking in stockpot, ribs may be finished in oven on a foil-lined cookie sheet at 350°F for 30 minutes, basting several times and turning ribs at least twice.

Gypsy Gourmet

For extra zing, add to the soda pop mixture:

- Few dashes hot sauce
- 2 tablespoons cumin

Soda Pop Beef Ribs

Serves 2–4, or 1 hungry truck driver

2 liters regular (not diet) orange soda (cola works, too)

2 bay leaves

1 clove garlic, skin on

3–4 pounds beef ribs or short ribs on the bone

2 cups Chipotle Orange BBQ sauce, Chapter 4, or your favorite BBQ sauce

1. In a large stockpot, bring soda, bay leaves, and garlic to a boil.

2. Add ribs. If liquid does not cover ribs, add water or more soda to just cover them.

3. Cover pot and simmer on medium heat for 30 minutes.

4. Remove ribs from pot and baste ribs with BBQ sauce.

5. Grill on medium heat for 8–10 minutes, basting 3–4 times. Serve.

Southwestern Pork Tenderloin

Serves 2–6 (see Tip)

2–3 pounds pork tenderloins

1 tablespoon chili powder

1 teaspoon cumin

¼ teaspoon salt

Pinch of cayenne pepper

1 teaspoon garlic powder

2 tablespoons cooking oil

1. Wash and pat pork tenderloins dry and set aside.

2. Combine chili powder, cumin, salt, cayenne, and garlic powder in a small bowl. Mix thoroughly and set aside.

3. Place oil on plate, then roll and coat tenderloin in it.

4. Sprinkle on chili powder rub and let coated meat sit for 15 minutes.

5. Preheat oven to 375°F.

6. Bake 25–35 minutes to desired doneness.

Rub can be saved in airtight container or baggie up to 2 months. Rub will cover 2 pork tenderloins (enough for 4–6 people), 4–6 large pork chops (4–6 people), or 3–4 pounds country style ribs (3–4 people).

Any apples
will suffice for
this recipe but if
you want apples
to remain intact,
use Cortland's,
Braeburn, or Gala
apples as they remain
firm during cooking.

Sweet-and-Sour Pork Chops with Sautéed Cabbage and Apples

Servings 2–4

½ cup sugar

¾ cup water

2 tablespoons garlic, put through press

¼ cup cider vinegar

2 tablespoons soy sauce

1 tablespoon Dijon mustard, optional

1 apple, peeled and cored, sliced thin

2 onions, sliced thin (about 2 cups)

½ head cabbage, shredded (4–5 cups)

½ stick of butter

2–4 pounds pork chops

Salt and pepper to taste

1. In a medium-sized bowl, mix sugar, water, garlic, vinegar, soy sauce, and mustard (if desired), to make sweet-and-sour sauce. Set aside.

2. In a large bowl, toss together the apple, onions, and cabbage. Set aside.

3. In a 12" skillet, melt butter. Season chops with salt and pepper, then brown in butter on both sides.

4. Remove chops from pan and set aside.

5. In same pan, sauté cabbage, apples, and onions for 4–5 minutes.

6. Return pork chops to pan.

7. Simmer on medium-low heat, uncovered, for 30 minutes, turning chops once or twice.

8. Cover and cook another 15–20 minutes, till done. Serve with sweet-and-sour sauce.

Pot Roast with Pan Gravy

Serves 2–4

2–4 pound chuck roast

Pepper to taste

3 tablespoons olive oil

3 onions, chopped

2 carrots, peeled and chopped

1 rib celery, chopped

5 cloves garlic, put through press

10 ounces beef stock or consommé

1 14-ounce can chicken stock

2 cups water

2 bay leaves

3 sprigs thyme or 1 teaspoon dried

1 tablespoon ketchup or tomato paste

Gypsy
Gourmet

For a more flavorful sauce, add ⅓ cup red wine or 2 tablespoons ruby port or brandy to the pan drippings.

1. Preheat oven to 325°F, arranging racks to accommodate pot.

2. Pat the roast dry and season with pepper. Set aside.

3. Heat oil in a large Dutch oven or 6–8 quart stock pot with lid to medium heat. Brown roast on all sides.

4. Add onions, vegetables, garlic, stock, water, bay leaves, and thyme. Bring to a boil.

5. Cover and place in oven.

6. Cook for 3–3½ hours, turning meat 2–3 times. Meat is done when knife goes through meat easily.

7. Remove meat from pan and place on platter.

8. Degrease pan drippings, if needed, by skimming fat off with spoon. Remove bay leaves and thyme sprigs. Return pan to stove top.

9. Add tomato paste and a little stock or water, if needed.

10. Simmer and reduce drippings on medium heat, 7–10 minutes. For a smoother gravy, strain before serving.

11. Season to taste. Serve pan drippings over slices of beef.

If you have time, cover ribs in plastic wrap and refrigerate 4–6 hours (make sure to remove plastic wrap before cooking).

Uncle Behoovie's Slow-Cooked Ribs with Vinegar Dipping Sauce

Serves 4–6

2 full racks pork ribs (not recommended for baby backs)

2 tablespoons garlic powder

½ cup packed brown sugar

2 teaspoons salt

2 teaspoons pepper

1 tablespoon paprika

2 teaspoons chili powder

1 recipe Vinegar Dipping Sauce, Chapter 4

1. Wash and pat ribs dry. Set aside.

2. In a medium bowl, blend remaining ingredients together. *Note*: Rub will keep sealed in covered container up to 2 months.

3. Coat ribs in rub and pat firmly.

4. Preheat oven to 325°F. Cover ribs in tightly sealed layers of foil. Place rib packets on foil-lined rimmed baking sheets or use disposable foil cooking sheets for easy clean up. Cook 2–2½ hours, turning ribs once.

5. Remove ribs from oven, loosen foil to let out steam, then let ribs rest 30 minutes.

6. Unwrap ribs, place on cutting board, and carve between bones. Serve with Vinegar Dipping Sauce, Chapter 4.

Pork Cutlets with Dipping Sauce

Serves 4

1 tablespoon soy sauce

6 tablespoons water, divided

2 teaspoons garlic, put through press

1½ pounds pork cutlets, pounded thin

½ cup all-purpose flour

2 eggs

½ teaspoon salt

½ teaspoon pepper

2½ cups bread crumbs

2–3 cups cooking oil

1 recipe Chipotle Dipping Sauce, Chapter 4, Sweet Sauce, Chapter 4, or your favorite

Gypsy Gourmet

Try using Bull-Dog Vegetable & Fruit Sauce (Tonkatsu) from Japan for dipping. This is a sweetened, salty, spicy tomato fruit sauce from Japan, used for dipping fried meat cutlets, seafood, or vegetables.

1. Whisk together soy sauce, 2 tablespoons water, and garlic in a shallow dish. Add pork cutlets and marinate 15–20 minutes.

2. Put flour in a small dish and set aside.

3. In another small dish, whisk together eggs, 4 tablespoons of water, salt, and pepper. Set aside.

4. On a plate, spread the bread crumbs and set aside.

continued on following page

5. Coat each cutlet in flour, then dip egg wash, then coat completely in bread crumbs. Set aside until all cutlets are coated.

6. Put oil in a 10" skillet (it should be about ⅓ full) on medium heat. Oil is ready when a drop of batter dropped into it sizzles.

7. Fry cutlets in batches of 2–3 at a time. Do not overcrowd the skillet. Cook till golden crispy, 2–3 minutes per side. Drain on paper-towel-lined plate.

8. Serve with dipping sauce.

Cuban Marinated Flank Steak with Lime Butter

Serves 4

8 cloves garlic, put through press

1 teaspoon soy sauce

Juice of 4 limes, about 8 tablespoons

½ teaspoon salt

¼ teaspoon black pepper

¼ cup olive oil

2–3 pounds flank steak, fat trimmed, washed and patted dry

1–2 tablespoons cooking oil

1 recipe Lime Butter, Chapter 4

1. Combine garlic, soy sauce, lime juice, salt, pepper, and olive oil in a re-sealable bag and mix well, then add steak.

2. Marinate steak in the refrigerator for 4–6 hours, or overnight.

3. Add cooking oil to 10" skillet and heat on high. Remove steak from marinade and sear on both sides, then reduce heat to medium.

4. Cook till desired doneness, about 4–5 minutes per side for medium rare.

5. Let rest for a few minutes before cutting into strips. Pour Lime Butter over steak and serve.

Steak can also be grilled. Sear over high heat on both sides, then reduce heat and cook till done.

Gypsy Gourmet

To add more kick to the marinade, add:

- 2 packages Sazón Goya with cilantro and achiote

- 1 teaspoon Maggi Seasoning in place of the soy sauce

- 1 teaspoon of ground cumin

- Juice of ½ lemon, about 1 tablespoon

- 2 tablespoons minced onion

You can also use pot roast or lamb shanks for this recipe.

Braised Chuck Roast with Onions

Serves 2

2½–3 pound chuck roast

Salt and pepper to taste

4 tablespoons olive oil, divided

2 whole, peeled, medium onions

4 whole garlic cloves

2 bay leaves

1 cup beef stock

1. Preheat oven to 375°F.

2. Season chuck roast with salt and pepper. Place roast in an oven-safe Dutch oven (or use a large skillet, then transfer to a roasting pan to cook in oven).

3. On medium heat, brown roast on all sides in 2 tablespoons oil.

4. Put garlic and onion in a medium bowl and coat with remaining olive oil. Place garlic and onions in the pan with the roast. Add bay leaves and stock.

5. Cover and bake for 30 minutes. Uncover, turning vegetables and basting roast with pan drippings. Cover and cook another 20 minutes.

6. Turn vegetables and cook uncovered another 25–30 minutes. Remove bay leaves and serve.

Gypsy Gourmet

To add flavor to this recipe, reduce stock to ½ cup and add ½ cup dry red wine with the stock. You can also add 2 parsnips, peeled and cut, with the onions and garlic.

Beef Stir-Fry

Serves 4

2 tablespoons cornstarch or flour

3 tablespoons warm water

¾ pound sirloin, cut into thin strips

2 tablespoons cooking oil, plus more if needed

6 cloves garlic, put through press

1 red or green pepper, seeded and cut into thin strips

1 cup red onion

½ cup chicken or vegetable stock

⅓ cup soy sauce

1. In a bowl, mix cornstarch or flour with water and set aside.

2. Heat oil in a wok or 10" skillet on high. Add beef and brown quickly. Drain beef and set beef aside.

3. Stir-fry garlic for 3–4 minutes, then set aside with beef.

4. Stir-fry red or green pepper and onion, adding a little more oil if needed. Add soy sauce and stock, then stir-fry 2–3 minutes.

5. Return beef and garlic to pan and stir-fry 1–2 minutes. Add cornstarch or flour mixture and heat until sauce thickens.

VARIATION

Gingered Beef Stir-Fry

Add 3 tablespoons fresh ginger, peeled and cut into julienne strips, with the red or green pepper and onion.

 Try replacing the cornstarch or flour as a thickener with arrow root powder. It has fewer calories and reheats silky, not clumpy, the next day.

Gypsy Gourmet

To mix it up a little, add eggplant to the stir-fry with the meat. Use 1 large Japanese eggplant or a small regular purple eggplant, cut into finger-size pieces. Also, try adding with the soy sauce and stock:

*   1 tablespoon, plus 2 teaspoons of oyster sauce
*   2 tablespoons sesame oil
*   3 scallions, white and green parts cut into 1-inch pieces
*   ½ teaspoon chili sauce or hot sauce

New England Boiled Dinner

Serves 6–8

5–7 pound smoked pork shoulder, bone in

5 cloves

8 cups water

½ cup yellow mustard

1 clove garlic, whole

2–3 celery sticks, cut to desired size

5 carrots, peeled and cut to desired size

1 cabbage, cored and cut in half

3–4 large potatoes, peeled and cut to desired size

5 medium onions, peeled and left whole

1. Rinse and pat dry the pork shoulder. Push the cloves into the pork shoulder.

2. In a large stockpot, add shoulder, water, mustard, and garlic. Bring to a boil.

3. Reduce heat to medium and simmer, covered, for 1 hour and 15 minutes.

4. Prepare vegetables. Add to stockpot with shoulder. Cover and cook 25–30 minutes, till vegetables are fork tender.

5. Remove the vegetables and serve separately.

Leftover ham makes delicious sandwiches and the bone can be used for flavoring pea soup.

Gypsy Gourmet

Serve your guests choices of mustard: grainy, Dijon, spicy brown, or yellow.

Spicy Enchiladas

Makes 8

½ pound beef steak strips, cut into small pieces,
or ground beef

2 tablespoons cooking oil

¼ teaspoon salt

Pepper to taste

½ cup onions, minced fine

5 cloves garlic, put through press

⅛ teaspoon cayenne pepper or hot sauce

2 tablespoons tomato paste or ketchup

8 yellow corn tortillas, 6" each

1 recipe Black Bean dip, Chapter 4, Worcestershire sauce
omitted (optional)

Gypsy Gourmet

For more flavor, add
to meat mixture
while cooking:

- 1 packet Sazón
  Goya seasoning
  with achiote

- 1½ tablespoons
  curry powder

- 2½ tablespoons
  cumin powder

- ⅛ teaspoon
  habanero powder

1. Preheat oven to 350°F.

2. In a medium skillet, brown meat in oil over medium heat.
   Season with salt and pepper. Add onions and garlic and
   sauté for 2–3 minutes. Add hot sauce and tomato paste and
   simmer 2–3 minutes. Set aside to cool

3. Place 1 tortilla on work surface. Add about 1–2 tablespoons
   meat filling per tortilla and 1 tablespoon bean dip (if
   desired). Fold tortilla sides in and roll from back to front.
   Repeat with each tortilla. Place on greased cookie sheet and
   cover with foil. Bake for 7–10 minutes.

4. Serve with Fresh Guacamole, Chapter 4, Fresh Mexican
   Salsa, Chapter 4, or your favorite hot sauce.

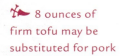 8 ounces of firm tofu may be substituted for pork

Pork and Green Bean Stir-Fry

Serves 2

½ pound pork (use ground pork meat or thin slices from a pork tenderloin)

1 tablespoon cooking oil

½ pound cut green beans

1 medium onion, sliced thin

3 cloves garlic, put through press

¼ cup water or chicken stock

1 tablespoon soy sauce

1. In a 12" skillet on medium-high heat, stir-fry pork in oil for 2–3 minutes. Remove pork from pan and set aside.

2. Add green beans and stir-fry 2–3 minutes.

3. Add onion and garlic and stir-fry 2 minutes.

4. Add water or stock and stir-fry till almost evaporated.

5. Return pork to pan and stir-fry 2–3 minutes.

6. Add soy sauce and stir-fry 2–3 minutes.

7. Serve immediately with rice.

Gypsy Gourmet

To add more kick to the stir-fry, add with the soy sauce:

- A pinch of hot chili flakes or ¼ teaspoon hot Asian chili sauce
- 1 tablespoon toasted sesame oil
- 2 tablespoons oyster sauce

Grilled Garlic Pork Chops

Serves 4

1 tablespoon garlic, put through a press

½ cup rice vinegar

¼ cup cooking oil

Dash of pepper

Pinch of salt

4 large pork chops

1. Whisk together all ingredients (except chops).

2. Place chops in a shallow dish and pour marinade over. Let marinate for 20–30 minutes.

3. Heat grill on high for ten minutes. Sear chops on each side. Then reduce heat to medium and cook to desired doneness, about 4–5 minutes per side for 1" thick chops. Turn off grill and rest meat with lid down, 3–5 minutes. Serve.

Jerk Pork

Serves 6–8

3 tablespoons of jerk seasoning

3 cups pineapple juice

2 tablespoons cooking oil

1 tablespoon garlic, put through press

Dash of black pepper

7–10 pound pork shoulder, butterflied and deboned (leave fat rind intact)

1. Combine ingredients (except for pork) in a re-sealable bag and mix well. Add pork and refrigerate overnight or up to 2 days, turning bag occasionally.

2. Preheat oven to 375°F.

3. Place pork, fat side up, in heavy duty foil roasting pan or line a roasting pan with foil. Cover tightly with foil.

4. Bake for 1 hour and 10 minutes.

5. Remove foil and continue baking 20–25 minutes, till fat rind gets brown and crispy.

6. Remove from oven and let meat rest 10–15 minutes before slicing.

7. Serve with hot sauce and Rice and Beans, Chapter 9.

Beef Stew with Corn and Potatoes

Serves 6–8

1½ pounds beef stew meat, such as chuck, cubed

2 tablespoons cooking oil

3½ cups onions, sliced

3 tablespoons garlic, put through press

6 cups water

2 10.5-ounce cans beef consommé or stock

1 teaspoon salt

¼ teaspoon pepper

1 teaspoon thyme leaves

2 bay leaves

3 large potatoes, peeled and cubed

2 ears corn (off cob) or 1 10-ounce can corn, drained

Gypsy Gourmet

For extra flavor, add ¾ cup red wine with the water.

1. In a large stockpot set on high, brown meat in oil. Remove meat and set aside.

2. Sauté onions and garlic till tender. Return meat to pan. Add water, consommé, salt, pepper, thyme, and bay leaves. Bring to a boil. Reduce heat to a simmer. Cook, uncovered, 45 minutes, till meat is somewhat tender.

3. Add potatoes and cook for 15 minutes, uncovered.

4. Add corn and cook 5–10 minutes until potatoes are fork tender. Remove bay leaves and serve.

Rub can be kept for 2 months in a sealed jar.

The Sugar Monster's Steak Rub

Serves 5–8, depending on appetite!

2 teaspoons dry mustard powder

4 tablespoons brown sugar, packed

1 teaspoon salt

1½ teaspoons black pepper

1 tablespoon, plus 1 teaspoon garlic powder

1 teaspoon cumin

2 teaspoons paprika

5 pounds steak of your choice: t-bone, fillet, sirloin, strips, rib eye, or London broil

1. Combine all ingredients (except steak) in a bowl and mix thoroughly.

2. Coat steak with mixture completely on all sides. If you have time, let steak rest overnight in a re-sealable bag.

3. Otherwise, cook immediately.

4. Grill to desired doneness. For 1" thick steaks, sear on hot grill 2–3 minutes per side, a little longer for thicker steaks. Reduce heat and cook additional 2–3 minutes per side for rare, longer for thicker steaks or more doneness. Let meat rest off direct heat for 5 minutes. Serve.

Hail Caesar Steak Tips

Serves 4

2–3 pounds sirloin or other beef steak tips

1 cup Caesar Salad Dressing, Chapter 4, or use bottled Caesar on hand and add the following:

> **3 cloves garlic, put through a press**
>
> **2 tablespoons Dijon mustard**
>
> **¼ teaspoon salt**
>
> **1 teaspoon pepper**

1. In a re-sealable gallon or larger size plastic bag, put the steak in, then the salad dressing (and other ingredients, if needed).

2. Squeeze out excess air and close bag. Marinate 30 minutes to 1 hour.

3. Grill to desired doneness. Sear 1" pieces of tips on each side for 2–3 minutes, then cook another 3–4 minutes on each side on medium heat, longer for more doneness. Let meat rest off direct heat for 5 minutes. Serve.

Gypsy Gourmet

For an extra level of flavor, add ¼ cup red wine to the salad dressing.

Balsamic Peppercorn Steak

Serves 4

🌶 Tougher cuts of beef like blade steaks, chuck, or London broil can be marinated overnight.

2 tablespoons soy sauce

2 teaspoons garlic powder or 3 garlic cloves, put through press

3 tablespoons olive oil

2 teaspoons pepper

2 tablespoons balsamic vinegar

2–4 pounds beef steak, such as sirloin, skirt, or London broil

1. Whisk together all ingredients (except steak) in a small bowl and set aside.

2. Place steak in a shallow dish and cover with marinade. Turn once or twice to coat.

3. Place in refrigerator and marinate for 30 minutes.

4. Grill to desired doneness. Sear 1" thick steaks on each side for 2–3 minutes, then cook another 3–4 minutes on each side on medium heat for rare steaks, longer for more doneness or thicker steaks. Remove meat from heat and let it rest for 5 minutes. Serve.

King Kong Hoobie Burgers

Makes 4–6 burgers

1½–2 pounds ground beef, 85 percent lean

½ teaspoon salt

¼ teaspoon pepper

1 egg

2 tablespoons water

4–6 slices cheese, if desired

1 sweet onion, sliced in thick slices

4–6 sesame seed buns, toasted

1. In a large bowl, combine ground beef, salt, pepper, egg, and water.

2. Form meat mixture into patties.

3. In a 10" nonstick skillet on medium-high, cook 2–3 patties at a time to desired doneness, about 4–5 minutes per side for medium doneness. Remove pan from heat and let burgers rest in pan for 5 minutes.

4. Top each burger with a slice of cheese, if desired. Let melt, then add onion slice. Serve on a toasted bun.

Gypsy Gourmet

For special flare, use slices of Gruyère or Compte cheese to top burgers. For extra kick, add to the meat mixture:

- 2 teaspoons chili powder
- 1 small red jalapeño, deseeded and chopped finely
- 1 small green jalapeño, deseeded and chopped finely

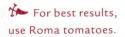 For best results, use Roma tomatoes.

Paper Thin Tomato Basil Pizzas

Serves 2

2 9" soft flour tortillas

2 tablespoons olive oil

1 6-ounce can tomato paste

1 teaspoon garlic powder

1 teaspoon dried oregano, optional

2 cups 6-cheese blend, shredded

3 tomatoes, seeded and cut into cubes

8 basil leaves thinly (julienne) cut

Crushed red chili pepper flakes (optional)

1 recipe Red Chili Garlic Oil, Chapter 4

1. Preheat oven to 450°F.

2. Brush both sides of tortillas with olive oil, place on baking sheet or on cookie sheet and cook in oven till crisp, turning once, about 2–3 minutes each side.

3. Remove pan from oven. Spread tortillas with tomato paste, sprinkle with garlic powder, and oregano, if desired. Top with cheese and cubed tomato.

4. Cook 4–5 minutes in oven, till cheese gets bubbly.

5. Top with basil leaves and chili pepper flakes (if desired). Top with Red Chili Garlic Oil, Chapter 4, and a sprinkle of pepper flakes. Cut and serve.

VARIATION

Sausage and Onion Pizza

Sauté 2 sweet Italian sausages (removed from casings) and one large chopped onion. Add to tortillas with cheese and tomato.

Grilled Sirloin Strips with Ginger Rum BBQ Sauce

Serves 4–6

Gypsy Gourmet

For more intense flavor, add to the BBQ sauce:

- 1 tablespoon, plus 1 teaspoon of cumin
- ½ cup molasses or hoisin sauce
- ⅛ teaspoon powdered clove
- ½ teaspoon chili powder
- ½ cup espresso coffee
- 2 tablespoons sugar
- ½ teaspoon coriander

1 6-ounce can of tomato paste

1 cup water

½ cup vinegar, preferably cider vinegar

½ teaspoon salt

⅛ teaspoon pepper

2 teaspoons garlic powder

¼ teaspoon cayenne pepper

2 tablespoons Dijon mustard

½ cup preserves of your choice; strawberry, peach, marmalade, or grape jelly

¼ cup white rum or regular rum

2 teaspoons fresh ginger, grated

4 pounds sirloin strips

1. Combine all Ginger Rum BBQ sauce ingredients (except steak) in a saucepan and simmer on low 30–35 minutes. Set aside to cool.

2. Turn grill on high. Sear meat for 2–3 minutes each side, then reduce heat to medium-low and cook for 4–5 minutes on each side with the lid down.

3. Lower heat and apply BBQ sauce several times on both sides as meat cooks (lid down) to desired doneness, about 5–7 minutes to get a nice glaze. Serve.

Stuffed Cabbage Leaves

Makes about 10–14 stuffed cabbage leaves

You can also use the meat-and-rice mixture to stuff green peppers.

1 large head green cabbage, about 4–5 pounds

2 tablespoons cooking oil

½ pound ground beef, 85 percent lean (or substitute ground pork, chicken, or turkey)

1 cup onion, puréed

1 tablespoon garlic, put through press

2 teaspoons pepper

1½ teaspoons salt

3 cups cooked white rice, packed

2–3 tablespoons water

2–3 cups Red Sauce, Chapter 4, or marinara sauce

Sour cream for garnish (optional)

1. Cover cabbage in plastic wrap and place on microwave-safe dish with core side up. Cook in microwave on high for 23 minutes.

2. Remove from microwave and let completely cool before removing plastic wrap, about 45 minutes to 1 hour.

3. When cool, cut center core out of cabbage and remove leaves, then set aside.

4. Add oil to a 10" skillet on medium heat. Add meat and brown, breaking apart meat as it cooks.

5. Add onion, garlic, pepper, and salt, and cook till tender.

6. Add cooked rice and water. Mix together and set aside.

7. Preheat oven to 350°F.

8. Grease a 10" baking pan.

9. Place 1 cabbage leaf on clean work surface. Place 2 tablespoons of meat-and-rice mixture in center of leaf.

10. Fold bottom edge toward mixture, then fold in sides. Roll forward, so that meat-and-rice mixture is contained inside the cabbage leaf.

11. Set rolled cabbage leaves in prepared baking dish.

12. Cover in Red Sauce or marinara sauce.

13. Cover dish with foil and bake for 35–45 minutes. Serve with sour cream garnish, if desired.

Three Bean and Beef Chili

Serves 8–10

Gypsy
Gourmet

3 pounds ground beef, 85 percent lean

3 tablespoons garlic, put through press

4 cups onion, chopped

3 tablespoons cooking oil

1 28-ounce can crushed tomato sauce

1 6-ounce can tomato paste

1 cup chicken or beef stock

¾ cup water

1 teaspoon salt

5 tablespoons chili powder

2 teaspoons oregano

3 15-ounce cans of beans, rinsed and drained. Choose your 3 bean options from black beans, bola rojas, pinto, dark red kidney, or navy beans

1 recipe Fresh Guacamole, Chapter 4, or Fresh Mexican Salsa, Chapter 4

For extra zing, add these ingredients after the meat has browned:

- 1 small red pepper, with ribs and seeds removed, then minced

- 3 tablespoons cumin

- 2 tablespoons sugar or honey

- 1 tablespoon chipotle sauce

- 3–4 dashes hot sauce

- ¼ cup tequila

1. In a large skillet, sauté beef, garlic, and onion in oil until meat is browned.

2. Add in tomato sauce, tomato paste, stock, water, salt, chili powder, oregano, and beans.

3. Simmer on low for about 35–40 minutes.

4. Serve topped with Fresh Guacamole, Chapter 4, or Fresh Mexican Salsa, Chapter 4.

CHAPTER 8

Seafood Dishes

Baked Fish with Crispy Garlic Bread Crumbs

Serves 2

5 tablespoons butter

⅔ cup bread crumbs

1 teaspoon garlic powder

¼ teaspoon salt

¼ teaspoon pepper

1–1½ pounds white fish, such as haddock, tilapia, hake, rock fish, or cod

Lemon wedges for squeezing

1 recipe Tartar Sauce, Chapter 4

Gypsy Gourmet

Add ¾ teaspoon dried thyme, oregano, paprika, or Italian seasoning to bread crumbs to add extra flavor.

1. Melt butter in microwave-safe bowl on high in 20-second intervals till melted.

2. Add bread crumbs, garlic powder, salt, and pepper. Stir.

3. Heat oven to 450°F for 10 minutes.

4. Place fish in baking dish and cover in crumb mixture. Bake uncovered for 10 minutes.

5. Turn heat off and rest fish in oven for 2 minutes.

6. Serve with lemon wedges and Tartar Sauce, Chapter 4.

Crab Cakes with Chipotle Dipping Sauce

Serves 6–8

½ cup mayonnaise

2 tablespoons Dijon mustard

1 teaspoon Worcestershire sauce

¼ teaspoon salt

¼ teaspoon pepper

2 teaspoons garlic powder

12 Ritz crackers, crumbled

1 egg

2 tablespoons cornstarch

1 tablespoon olive oil, preferably extra-virgin

1 tablespoon sugar

Juice of 1 lemon, about 2 tablespoons

1 pound fresh crab meat, squeezed dry and flaked (or substitute canned or frozen)

1 cup bread crumbs

½ cup cooking oil for frying

1 recipe Chipotle Dipping Sauce, Chapter 4

1. Mix all ingredients (except bread crumbs and cooking oil). Form this crab mixture into cakes and roll each cake in bread crumbs to coat.

continued on following page

> If you prefer fish cakes, substitute 1 pound of crab for haddock, cod, or hake.

Gypsy Gourmet

To kick up the flavor on this dish, add to the crab mixture:

- 3 scallions, white and green parts finely chopped
- 2 tablespoons flat leaf parsley, chopped fine
- 1 teaspoon Mirin cooking wine
- Few dashes Parrot hot sauce
- ¼ teaspoon smoked paprika
- 1 teaspoon of brined capers, squeezed dry and finely minced or ½ teaspoon of powdered capers

2. In a medium saucepan, heat cooking oil on medium heat. Test oil for readiness by placing a tip of a crab cake in the oil. Oil is ready when it sizzles. Fry crab cakes 5–7 minutes each, till slightly golden.

3. Serve immediately or keep warm in oven at 350°F. Serve warm with Chipotle Dipping Sauce, Chapter 4.

Marmalade Glazed Salmon

Serves 2 for dinner, 4 as an appetizer

2 tablespoons orange juice

¼ cup orange marmalade

½ teaspoon soy sauce

Pinch of cayenne pepper, optional

1–1½ pounds salmon

1. Preheat oven to 400°F.

2. In a small bowl, combine juice, marmalade, soy sauce, and cayenne (if desired). Set aside.

3. Place salmon in a greased 10" baking dish, skin side down.

4. Brush a thick layer of glaze over fish.

5. Bake uncovered for 8–10 minutes.

Gypsy Gourmet

For a fun garnish, slice 3–5 thin wheels from an orange, coat them with the glaze, and serve with the salmon.

Shrimp for a Prince

Serves 2, or 4 as an appetizer

1 10-ounce can tomato or tomato bisque soup

¾ cup chicken stock

1 tablespoon of cream sherry, sweet Marsala, sweet vermouth, or sugar

2 garlic cloves, put through press

½ cup cream or half-and-half

1 pound shrimp, peeled and deveined, preferably with tails on

1 box of linguini or fettuccini cooked al dente or 4 cups cooked rice

1. In a 10" skillet, heat tomato soup on medium.

2. Add stock, sherry, and garlic and simmer 4–5 minutes while stirring.

3. Add cream and shrimp. Simmer 4–5 minutes.

4. Add cooked pasta (or rice) to pan, toss and serve.

Gypsy Gourmet

For a bit of zing in the sauce, add:

- 1 tablespoon dried ground chorizo

- ½ teaspoon smoked paprika

- Garnish with chopped parsley or cilantro

Mussels for a King

Make sauce as above. Add 2–3 pounds of fresh cleaned mussels in place of shrimp. Cover mussels and simmer 5–7 minutes or until mussels open. Discard any mussels that do not open. Ladle into bowls, covering mussels with sauce. Serve with crusty warm bread.

Baked Fish for a Prince

Make sauce as above. Preheat oven to 450°F. Place 1½–2 pounds white fish in a baking dish. Cover fish with sauce. Top with 6–8 crumbled Ritz crackers. Dollop with 2–3 tablespoons butter, sliced thin. Bake 8–10 minutes. Turn heat off, let fish rest in oven 2–3 minutes. Serve with Tartar Sauce, Chapter 4.

Choose white fish such as tilapia, rock fish, sole, bass, perch, or cod.

Mexican Spiced Garlic Shrimp

Serves 2–3, or 4–6 as an appetizer

Gypsy Gourmet

To take this dish to an interesting place, add 1 tablespoon cumin, ⅛ teaspoon cayenne pepper, or 1–2 dashes hot sauce.

6 tablespoons butter

Juice of 4 limes, about 8 tablespoons

¾ teaspoon salt (omit salt if using salted butter)

1 tablespoon garlic, put through press

1–2 pounds shrimp

1. In a medium microwave-safe dish, melt butter on high (will take about 1–1½ minutes).

2. Add lime juice, salt (if needed), and garlic to dish. Mix.

3. Add shrimp and toss to coat. Marinate shrimp for 10–15 minutes.

4. Grill or broil shrimp for 3–4 minutes and serve.

Grilled Shrimp with Lemon Blackened Butter

Serves 2–3, or 4–6 as an appetizer

¾ **stick butter**

Juice of 1 lemon, about 2 tablespoons

2 tablespoons blackening seasoning

¼ **teaspoon salt (omit salt if using salted butter)**

2 pounds shrimp, peeled or unpeeled

1. In a small saucepan, heat butter and lemon together on medium heat, till butter melts.

2. Add blackening seasoning and salt (if needed). Simmer on low for 4–5 minutes, till bubbly.

3. Set aside, keeping butter warm but not hot.

4. Skewer shrimp and baste with sauce. Grill 2–3 minutes each side. Serve.

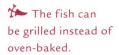 The fish can be grilled instead of oven-baked.

Cajun Fish

Serves 4–6

2–3 pounds fish fillets, such as mackerel, grouper, perch, catfish, blue, or striper (this seasoning will overpower more delicate fish such as flounder, haddock, or salmon)

½ cup mayonnaise

Pinch of salt

3 tablespoons blackening seasoning

1–2 lemons or limes cut into wedges for squeezing

1 recipe Tartar Sauce, Chapter 4

1. Preheat oven to 450°F for 10 minutes.

2. Line baking dish with greased foil.

3. Coat each fish fillet with a layer of mayonnaise and pinch of salt, then generously apply blackening seasoning. Place in foil-lined dish.

4. Bake for 8–10 minutes.

5. Turn off oven and let fish rest in oven for 2–4 minutes.

6. Serve with lemon or lime wedges and Tartar Sauce, Chapter 4.

Fried Fish

Serves 4–6

1½–2 pounds white fish of your choice: cod, tilapia, pollock, whiting, rock fish, haddock, or hake.

½ cup cornstarch (flour will work in a pinch)

1½ cups all-purpose flour

2 teaspoons pepper

½ teaspoon salt

1 tablespoon garlic powder

1 tablespoon baking soda

1 12-ounce can of ice-cold pale ale or 12 ounces of ice-cold water

2–3 cups oil

1 recipe Tartar Sauce, Chapter 4

1. Remove skin from fish. Cut into pieces about 2" × 5" and about ¾" thick. Coat in cornstarch and set aside.

2. In a large bowl, combine flour, pepper, salt, garlic powder, and baking soda. When ready to cook, add cold liquid to flour mix and whisk together.

3. Heat oil in large skillet (skillet should be ⅓ full) on medium-high. Oil is ready when a drop of batter added to it sizzles. Coat fish in batter and shake off excess. Place fish into hot oil, 2–3 pieces at a time. Do not overcrowd the skillet. Cook for 3–4 minutes on each side, turning when golden.

4. Drain on paper-towel-lined plate.

5. Serve with Tartar Sauce, Chapter 4.

Peppered Cod with Ranch Dressing and Ritz Cracker Crumbs

Serves 2

6–8 crumbled Ritz crackers

1½ pounds cod, washed and patted dry

¼ cup ranch dressing

Dash pepper

Pinch garlic powder or paprika

2 tablespoons butter or olive oil

1 recipe Tartar Sauce, Chapter 4

1. Preheat oven to 450°F.

2. Put Ritz crackers in a baggie and crush with rolling pin till they reach the consistency of fine bread crumbs. Set aside.

3. Coat fish in ranch dressing and place in greased baking pan.

4. Season with pepper and garlic powder or paprika.

5. Cover in Ritz cracker crumbs and top with pats of butter or sprinkle with olive oil. Bake 8–10 minutes.

6. Serve with Tartar Sauce, Chapter 4.

Grilled Littlenecks with Lemon Chili Sauce

Serves 4–6

3–5 pounds littleneck clams

½ cup lemon juice

¾ stick butter

2 teaspoons Asian chili sauce

½ teaspoon salt

1. Scrub clams clean and set aside.

2. In a saucepan, bring lemon juice to a boil. Reduce heat to a low simmer.

3. Add in butter, chili sauce, and salt. Simmer on low for 5–7 minutes.

4. Preheat grill on high heat for 7 minutes.

5. Place clams on hottest part of grill and close cover. Clams are done when shells open, about 6–10 minutes. Discard any clams that do not open.

6. Remove clams and place on platter. Serve with warm Lemon Chili Sauce.

Mussels with Thyme Butter

Serves 2

2–3 pounds mussels

1 stick butter

2 large bay leaves

2 cups clam broth

1½ tablespoons garlic, minced

8–10 sprigs fresh thyme

Gypsy Gourmet

For a more flavorful broth, add ¼ cup dry vermouth or dry white wine. Add 1–2 dashes hot sauce for a more complex flavor.

1. Clean mussels and set aside.

2. In a large saucepan, melt butter. Add bay leaves, clam broth and garlic. Bring to a boil.

3. Add in thyme sprigs and mussels. Cover and simmer on medium heat for 5–7 minutes, till mussels open.

4. Serve with crusty bread.

Pan Seared Scallops

Serves 2

1¼ pounds of fresh scallops

¼ cup cooking wine

3–4 tablespoons cooking oil

1 recipe Tartar Sauce, Chapter 4

1. Rinse scallops, drain.

2. Put wine and scallops in a small bowl, and let marinate at least 30 minutes (or overnight).

3. When ready to cook, drain scallops well and pat dry.

4. Melt butter in a 10" skillet on medium-high heat.

5. Quickly pan sear scallops 2–3 minutes on each side.

6. Remove from heat and rest scallops in pan for 3–4 minutes before serving.

7. Serve with Tartar Sauce, Chapter 4.

I like to use Mirin as my cooking wine. Mirin is a Japanese sweet rice cooking wine with low alcohol content. It imparts a subtle sweetness to seafood dishes, sauces, and marinades.

Salmon with Shallot Butter

Serves 2, or 4–6 as an appetizer

2 tablespoons green peppercorn mustard or Dijon mustard

2 medium shallots, minced

¼ teaspoon salt

¼ teaspoon pepper

5 tablespoons butter, softened

1–2 pounds salmon, skin removed

1. Preheat oven to 450°F for 10 minutes.

2. Combine mustard, shallots, salt, and pepper together and add to softened butter.

3. Spread all over salmon.

4. Place fish in a baking dish on the top rack of oven and cook 8–9 minutes.

5. Turn oven off and let fish rest in oven for 4 minutes. Serve.

Shrimp Puffs

Serves 2

1 pound fresh shrimp, cleaned and deveined

¼ cup cornstarch

1½ cups all-purpose flour

1½ teaspoons baking powder

1 teaspoon salt

¼ teaspoon pepper

¼ teaspoon paprika

¼ teaspoon garlic powder

2–3 cups cooking oil

10–12 ounces cold water or light ale (or substitute sparkling water)

1 recipe Tarter Sauce, Chapter 4

Lemon wedges for garnish, if desired

Gypsy Gourmet

For a more flavorful recipe, marinate shrimp in ¼ cup cooking wine, preferably Mirin, for 10–15 minutes before placing in batter and frying.

1. Put shrimp and cornstarch in a re-sealable plastic bag and shake to coat shrimp.

2. In a large mixing bowl, add flour, baking powder, salt, pepper, paprika, and garlic powder.

3. Heat cooking oil in a 10" skillet (it should be about ⅓ full) on medium-high heat.

4. Add cold liquid to flour mixture and whisk together. Mixture will be slightly bubbly. Note: Batter is only good for 20–30 minutes after liquid has been added.

continued on following page

5. Carefully test oil by dropping in one drop of batter. If droplet of batter sizzles and goes to top quickly, the oil is ready for frying.

6. Place 4–5 shrimp in batter and shake off excess. Fry in batches of 4–5 at a time. Don't overcrowd the skillet. Drain on paper-towel-lined plates.

7. Serve with Tarter Sauce, Chapter 4, and lemon wedges.

Salmon Avocado Salad

Serves 4–6

2 14.75-ounce cans salmon, drained, picked over to remove bones, and squeezed dry

Juice of 3 lemons, about 6 tablespoons, separated into 2 equal amounts

¼ cup olive oil

1 teaspoon salt

¼ teaspoon pepper

2 ripe avocados, mashed

1. Flake salmon in bowl and add half of lemon juice.

2. Whisk remaining lemon juice with oil, salt, and pepper.

3. Combine salmon, lemon juice mixture, and avocados. Chill for 15 minutes.

4. Serve over greens or stuff into pita bread.

Shrimp and Angel Hair Pasta

Serves 2–4

Gypsy Gourmet

To make the meal extra-special, add 2–3 medium plum tomatoes, seeded and diced, just before serving. To spice up the broth, add ¼ teaspoon of crushed hot pepper flakes and 1 tablespoon fresh thyme leaves, at the same time you add the pasta.

1 pound jumbo shrimp, peeled and deveined, tails on

6 cloves garlic, put through press

7 tablespoons olive oil

1 pound angel hair pasta, cooked al dente

¾ cup chicken stock or clam broth

Salt and pepper to taste

1 recipe Thyme Garlic Oil, Chapter 4, or Red Chili Garlic Oil, Chapter 4.

1. In a large skillet, sauté garlic in olive oil.

2. Add shrimp and sauté 2–3 minutes.

3. Add pasta and stock and toss, then simmer till most of liquid is absorbed.

4. Salt and pepper to taste. Serve with Thyme Garlic Oil, Chapter 4, or Red Chili Garlic Oil, Chapter 4.

 For tastier shrimp, soak them in this brine for ½ hour before cooking:

- 1½ cups water
- 1 tablespoon salt
- 1 tablespoon sugar

Shrimp Pad Thai Noodles

Serves 2

8 ounces rice stick noodles

3 large eggs, scrambled and set aside

4 cloves garlic, put through press

3 tablespoons cooking oil

4 tablespoons lemon juice

3 tablespoons soy sauce or fish sauce

1 teaspoon hot sauce

½ pound shrimp, peeled and deveined, with tails on

4 tablespoons roasted, unsalted peanuts, chopped; divided into equal halves

¼ cup water, if needed

1. Soak rice noodles in warm water for 15 minutes, then drain and set aside.

2. In a large skillet, sauté garlic in oil for 1–2 minutes.

3. Add noodles to pan and toss. Slowly add in lemon juice, soy sauce or fish sauce, hot sauce, shrimp, and half of peanuts. Toss while cooking for 4–5 minutes. Test noodles for tenderness. Add in a small amount of water if needed.

4. Add eggs and toss again. Cook another 2–3 minutes.

5. Top with remaining peanuts and serve.

Gypsy Gourmet

Add some extra kick to this recipe by adding 1 teaspoon white wine vinegar or cane vinegar with the lemon juice. You can also add ½ cup bean sprouts and 4 chopped scallions with the eggs. Consider adding 2 tablespoons chopped cilantro as a topping, and lemon or lime wedges as a garnish.

Shrimp and Peas over Pasta in Spiced Garlic Cream Sauce

Serves 4

Gypsy Gourmet

To add extra zing to this recipe, add 1 tablespoon Asian chili sauce to the butter as it's being melted.

1 pound pasta, preferably ribbon pasta (substitute fettuccine or similar pasta)

6 tablespoons butter

8–12 large raw shrimp, peeled and deveined, with tails on

½ cup cream

¼ teaspoon salt

Dash pepper

¼ cup grated Parmesan cheese

½ cup peas, fresh or frozen

1 tablespoon Asian chili sauce or 1 recipe Thyme Garlic Oil, Chapter 4

1. Cook pasta per package instructions for al dente. Set aside.

2. In a 10" skillet, melt butter, then sauté shrimp for 2–3 minutes.

3. Add in cooked pasta, cream, salt, and pepper and simmer 2–4 minutes.

4. Add cheese and peas. Simmer another 2–3 minutes.

5. Serve with Asian chili sauce or Thyme Garlic Oil, Chapter 4.

Spicy Mexican Tuna Salad

Serves 2–4

10 ounces canned tuna, drained and flaked

2 green jalapeños chopped fine, or 1 green and 1 red

2 tablespoons onion, chopped fine

½ cup mayonnaise

¼ teaspoon salt

¼ teaspoon pepper

Gypsy Gourmet

To spice up this recipe, add 1½ teaspoons cumin powder to the mix.

1. In a small bowl, mix together all ingredients.

2. Serve in sandwiches or stuff in garden tomatoes.

3. Keep covered in the refrigerator for 2–3 days.

CHAPTER 9

Vegetarian Dishes

Short on time? Try this short cut. Use your favorite commercial brand of macaroni and cheese and follow manufacturer's stovetop cooking instructions. While cooking: add ½ cup corn, ¼ cup peas, and 1 red and 1 green seeded jalapeño, minced fine (wear gloves while mincing).

Confetti Macaroni and Cheese

Serves 8–10

1 pound of your favorite pasta: small shells, elbows, or rotini

6 tablespoons butter, divided equally

1 cup bread crumbs

¼ tablespoon pepper

3 tablespoons flour

2 cups milk, divided equally

4 cups 6-cheese blend, shredded, divided equally

1 10–12-ounce package frozen corn, drained, or 3 ears fresh corn, kernels removed

½ cup peas, fresh or frozen

4 jalapeños, (2 red and 2 green if you want extra color), seeded and minced fine (use gloves for this step) or ¾ teaspoon hot sauce

1. Cook pasta in boiling water for 3 minutes only. Rinse in cold water and drain.

2. Preheat oven to 375°F.

3. In a small microwave-safe bowl, melt 3 tablespoons butter. Mix in bread crumbs and set aside.

4. In a saucepan on medium-low, melt 3 tablespoons butter with pepper.

5. Add flour and whisk together 7–8 minutes till thick paste forms.

6. Add in 1 cup milk and cook till mixture slightly thickens.

7. Add in half of cheese. Cook till melted.

8. In large oven-safe dish, place pasta, corn, peas, jalapeños, and rest of cheese. Mix.

9. Pour remainder of milk over pasta mixture.

10. Add cheese mixture and blend.

11. Top with bread crumbs and bake for 30–35 minutes until crumbs are golden and pasta is bubbly. Serve.

Curry Quinoa

Serves 4

Gypsy Gourmet

For a bit more zing, replace the olive oil with walnut oil, and add ¼ cup raisins.

1 cup quinoa, cooked

2 tablespoons olive oil, preferably extra-virgin

1 tablespoon maple syrup or honey

1 tablespoon water

2 teaspoons curry powder

½ teaspoon garlic powder

¼ cup unsalted pumpkin seeds, pecans, or walnuts

Mix all ingredients together thoroughly and serve.

Broccoli Tofu Stir-Fry with Hoisin Glaze

Serves 2

½ **pound broccoli**

2 tablespoons cooking oil

8 ounces firm tofu, drained and cubed

3 garlic cloves, put through press

2 tablespoons soy sauce

2 tablespoons hoisin sauce, or increase soy sauce by 2 tablespoons

¼ **cup water**

1. Cut broccoli to even-sized pieces. Place in bowl.

2. Cover and microwave on high 2 minutes, or steam for 3 minutes.

3. In a 12" skillet or wok on high, add oil.

4. Add broccoli and stir quickly 2–3 minutes.

5. Add tofu, garlic, soy sauce, hoisin, and water. Stir 2–3 minutes and serve.

Gypsy Gourmet

For a special Asian flare, use peanut oil in place of the cooking oil, and add 1 tablespoon toasted sesame oil and ½ teaspoon Asian chili sauce just before serving.

Cut tofu with your favorite shaped cookie cutters. Tofu cut in a Valentine's Day heart shape and served with red chili sauce makes a stunning appetizer for a loved one! Christmas tree shapes are fun for holidays—and don't forget animal shapes for kids (serve with honey-mustard dipping sauce).

Gypsy Gourmet

For an extra tasty marinade, use toasted sesame oil in place of cooking oil and add 2 tablespoons rice vinegar and 1 tablespoon freshly grated ginger. If you want extra extra crispy tofu, use panko bread crumbs instead of flour. Add 1 tablespoon white or black (or both) sesame seeds to bread crumbs for extra flavor.

Fried Tofu with Sweet Chili Sauce

Serves 2–4

2 tablespoons soy sauce

2 garlic cloves, put through press

3 tablespoons cooking oil, divided

1 pound firm tofu, cut into slices ½ inch thick

3 tablespoons flour

1 scallion, sliced thin, both white and green part (optional)

1 recipe Sweet Chili Sauce, Chapter 4, or your favorite sweet chili sauce

1. Whisk together soy sauce, garlic, and 1 tablespoon oil. Place in a shallow 10" dish. Add tofu and marinate 10–15 minutes, turning once.

2. Add the remainder of oil to a 10" skillet and heat on medium. Oil is ready when small piece of tofu dropped in sizzles.

3. Drain tofu.

4. Add flour to a shallow dish and dip tofu in flour (this step adds extra crispy goodness!).

5. Fry tofu till just brown, 1–2 minutes per side.

6. Serve with Sweet Chili Sauce, Chapter 4, and garnish with scallions (if desired).

Spinach Fettuccine Alfredo

Serves 2

1 pound fettuccini pasta, cooked al dente (linguini or thick egg noodles may be substituted)

½ stick butter

1¼ cups heavy cream

½ cup vegetable stock or chicken stock

1 cup grated Parmesan or other hard grating cheese

1 cup spinach, stems removed, chopped

¼ teaspoon nutmeg, optional

Salt and pepper to taste

1. Boil pasta per manufacturer's instructions in salted water. Drain and keep warm.

2. In a 12" skillet, melt butter on medium-low heat.

3. Add cream and stock and simmer on medium-low heat for 4–5 minutes.

4. Add pasta and cheese. Toss.

5. Add spinach, nutmeg, salt, and pepper. Toss and serve immediately.

Heat oven to 200°F and place plates or bowls inside oven for 10 minutes. That will keep pasta warm while eating.

Gypsy Gourmet

For a change of pace, ¼ cup peas or ½ cup chopped arugula may added in place of spinach.

Potato Salad

Serves 6–8

5 quarts water

2 tablespoons salt

5 pounds potatoes

1¼ cups mayonnaise

½ teaspoon pepper

1½ teaspoons salt

1 tablespoon vinegar

½ teaspoon garlic powder

1 medium onion, chopped

Gypsy Gourmet

For extra tang, substitute ½ cup mayonnaise and ¾ cup sour cream for the 1¼ cup mayonnaise. At the end, add in:

- 1 8.5-ounce can of peas, drained
- 2–3 scallions, green and white parts sliced
- 3 tablespoons parsley, minced

1. Bring water and salt to a boil in a large stockpot on medium-high heat.

2. Reduce heat. Add whole potatoes, cover and cook for 20–25 minutes until fork tender.

3. Cool potatoes in bowl of cold water.

4. Cut potatoes to desired-size pieces and add to large bowl.

5. In a medium bowl, mix together mayonnaise, pepper, salt, vinegar, garlic powder, and onion.

6. Add to potatoes and mix together.

7. Chill and serve.

Egg, Pea, and Potato Salad

Hard-boil 4–5 eggs. Cool, peel, chop eggs in desired pieces and add to salad.

Southwestern Chipotle Corn and Potato Salad

Omit vinegar from original recipe and add:

- 1 10-ounce can corn, drained
- 1 teaspoon chipotle sauce
- 1 tablespoon sugar
- Juice of 1 lime, about 2 tablespoons
- 2 tablespoons chopped cilantro

Summer Vegetable Medley

Serves 6–8

You can use 4 cups cooked rice instead of the pasta.

1 box orzo pasta or another small pasta such as elbows or small shells

1 cup grape tomatoes

1 medium red onion, cubed (or substitute any onion)

10 ounces frozen mixed vegetables (the more colors, the prettier!)

1 small red pepper, cut into tiny squares (green works but it's not as colorful!)

5–6 tablespoons olive oil, divided

3 cloves garlic, put through press

1 teaspoon salt

1 tablespoon vinegar, preferably wine vinegar

Juice of 1 lemon

1 tablespoon of water

1. Cook pasta per manufacturer's instructions in salted water.

2. Preheat oven to 375°F.

3. Combine onion, mixed vegetables, and pepper on a nonstick cookie sheet. Toss with small amount of oil and bake 10–12 minutes, turning once. Vegetables should be al dente. Remove from oven. Cool.

4. In a small bowl, whisk together garlic, salt, vinegar, lemon juice, rest of oil, and water. Set aside. Add pasta and vegetables to large bowl. Toss with dressing and serve.

Gypsy Gourmet

For more flavors, add to the mixed vegetables:

- 1 small zucchini, sliced thin

- 1 small summer squash, sliced thin

- 1 cup broccoli florets

- ¼ cup toasted pine nuts, walnuts, or pecans

- Garnish with 2 tablespoons fresh-snipped chives or 2 tablespoons minced flat leaf parsley

Sautéed Swiss Chard & Cannelloni Beans

Serves 4–6

1 15-ounce can cannelloni beans, drained and rinsed (navy, fava, chick peas, or pintos can be substituted)

3 garlic cloves, put through press

3 tablespoons olive oil

3–4 cups chopped Swiss chard, stems and leaves

½ cup chicken or vegetable stock

Salt and pepper to taste

1. In a 10" skillet, sauté garlic and beans in oil on medium heat.

2. Add chard and continue to sauté 3–4 minutes.

3. Add stock and reduce heat to low. Simmer, uncovered, for 8–10 minutes.

4. Season with salt and pepper to taste and serve.

Gypsy Gourmet

Look for rainbow Swiss chard (available with red, yellow, white stems) if you like color on the plate. Beet, turnip greens, fresh leaf spinach, or mustard greens can also be sautéed in place of Swiss chard.

Spicy Maple Cinnamon Sweet Potatoes

Serves 4–6

2 pounds cooked sweet potatoes

¾ stick butter

¼ teaspoon salt (omit if using salted butter)

1 tablespoon maple syrup or brown sugar, more if you like sweeter

½ teaspoon cinnamon

Pinch of habanero powder or ⅛ teaspoon cayenne pepper (optional)

In a large bowl, mash all ingredients together. Serve warm.

VARIATIONS

Sweet Potatoes with Cardamom

Replace maple syrup and cinnamon with 1 teaspoon cardamom powder.

Chipotle Orange Sweet Potatoes

Replace maple syrup and cinnamon with 1 teaspoon chipotle sauce and 6 ounces of frozen orange juice.

Eggplant Pie

Serves 4–6

1½–2 pounds eggplant, sliced ¼ inch thick with skin on

1½ cups ricotta cheese, divided equally

1 egg

1 teaspoon garlic powder

½ teaspoon salt

½ teaspoon pepper

1 teaspoon oregano

2 cups grated cheese, such as mozzarella or 6-cheese blend, divided equally

2 cups Red Sauce, Chapter 4, or marinara sauce

1. Preheat oven to 350°F.

2. Lightly grease a nonstick cookie sheet. Place sliced eggplant pieces on sheet and cook 12 minutes, turning once. Cool.

3. In a medium bowl, blend ricotta with egg, garlic powder, salt, pepper, and oregano till well mixed. Set aside.

4. Lightly grease a 9" or 10" square baking pan. Put ½ of eggplant in bottom of baking dish. Layer with ½ grated cheese, 1 cup Red Sauce, Chapter 4, and ½ of ricotta mixture. Layer with remaining eggplant, ricotta, and Red Sauce. Bake in center of oven 35–40 minutes.

5. Top with remaining grated, mozzarella, or blended cheese and return to oven for another 3–5 minutes, until cheese is melted. Remove from oven and let cool before cutting and serving.

Mozzarella balls, called bocconcini, are available in the cheese section of the grocery store, or in Italian markets. Regular mozzarella can be used, if cut into small chunks.

Mozzarella Salad with Sun-Dried Tomatoes

Serves 6–8

3 cups bite-size mozzarella balls, drained

½ cup sun-dried tomatoes in oil

5 cloves garlic, put through press

¼ cup olive oil

Juice of 1 lemon, about 2 tablespoons

⅛ teaspoon salt

Dash pepper

2 cups fresh basil leaves

1. Put mozzarella balls in a large salad bowl.

2. In food processor, combine sun-dried tomatoes, garlic, olive oil, lemon juice, salt, pepper, and basil. Process till mixture forms a paste. Toss with mozzarella balls.

3. Let rest for 30 minutes before serving. Serve at room temperature.

Roasted Cauliflower with Gorgonzola Cream Sauce and Toasted Walnuts

Serves 4–6

1 large head cauliflower, cut into florets

2 tablespoons olive oil

Salt and pepper to taste

1 recipe Gorgonzola Cream Sauce, Chapter 4

3 tablespoons chopped, toasted walnuts

1. Preheat oven to 375°F.

2. In a large bowl, combine cauliflower and oil and toss. Add salt and pepper to taste.

3. Transfer to a cookie sheet and bake for 15–18 minutes, till tender.

4. Cover cauliflower with Gorgonzola Cream Sauce, Chapter 4, and top with toasted walnuts. Serve warm.

Spicy Buttered Succotash

Serves 6–8

1 stick butter

1 tablespoon hot sauce or ¼ teaspoon cayenne pepper

16 ounces corn (canned or frozen) or 3 ears, kernels off cob

1 pound bag frozen lima beans (shelled edamame can be substituted)

½ cup chicken stock or vegetable stock

¼ teaspoon salt

1. In 10" skillet, melt butter and add hot sauce. Cook 2–3 minutes.

2. Add in corn, lima beans, stock, and salt. Simmer for 8–10 minutes.

3. Serve.

Potato Omelet

Serves 4–6

6 large eggs

2 tablespoons water

1 tablespoon Parmesan cheese, grated

¼ teaspoon salt

Dash pepper

3 tablespoons onion, minced

2 tablespoons olive oil

1 medium Yukon potato cooked, peeled, and mashed

1 cup tomatoes, diced (use red and yellow tomatoes for extra color), optional

1 recipe Red Chili Garlic Oil, Chapter 4, or sour cream

1. Preheat oven to 400°F.

2. In medium bowl, whisk together eggs, water, cheese, salt, and pepper. Set aside.

3. In a small skillet, sauté onion in oil till translucent. Set aside.

4. Lightly grease an 8" square baking pan. Add egg mixture, mashed potato, tomatoes, and sautéed onions to baking pan. Bake 10–12 minutes till firm.

5. Serve with a spoonful of tomatoes (if desired) and sour cream or Red Chili Garlic Oil, Chapter 4.

Vegetable Fried Rice

Serves 4

Gypsy Gourmet

To add extra flavor to this recipe:

- Include ¼ teaspoon five-spice powder in soy sauce mixture.

- Add ¼ pound meat or seafood of your choice. Stir-fry the meat till cooked in a small amount of oil, then set aside and add in with the rice, then sauté as directed.

- Add ½ cup fresh or frozen peas in with the rice and sauté as directed.

- Toss in 1 tablespoon fresh grated ginger, 2 scallions (white and green parts thinly sliced), and 1½ cups of rinsed bean sprouts to the saucepan just before serving.

1 tablespoon soy sauce

3 tablespoons water, divided

3 eggs

2 tablespoons cooking oil, divided equally

1 tablespoon garlic, put through press

1¼ cups onion, chopped

2½–3 cups cooked rice (don't use sticky or sushi rice, as it will not fry properly)

1 recipe Sweet Sauce, Chapter 4, or plum sauce or duck sauce

1. In a small bowl, whisk together 2 tablespoons water and soy sauce. Set aside.

2. In another small bowl, whisk together eggs and water.

3. In a large skillet, heat 1 tablespoon oil to medium and cook eggs till scrambled. Set aside.

4. Add remaining oil to skillet and sauté garlic and onions till translucent.

5. Add rice, soy sauce mixture, and scrambled eggs. Sauté 2–3 minutes. Serve with Sweet Sauce, Chapter 4, or plum sauce or duck sauce.

Rice and Beans

Serves 4–6

1½ cups rice

1¾ cups chicken or vegetable stock

2 tablespoons olive oil

1 medium onion, chopped fine

1 tablespoon garlic, put through a press

Dash pepper

¼ teaspoon salt

1 15-ounce can black beans, dark kidney beans, or pigeon beans, rinsed and drained

1. Place rice, stock, and oil into a large saucepan and cook, per rice package instructions.

2. Add in onion, garlic, pepper, salt, and beans. Cook until heated thoroughly.

VARIATIONS

Vegetable Rice

Omit the beans and add 1 10-ounce package frozen mixed vegetables to the mix.

Rice with Peas and Corn

Omit beans and add ½ cup frozen or fresh corn and ½ cup frozen or fresh peas.

Gypsy Gourmet

Add 3 packets of Sazón Goya with cilantro and achiote to the mix. This turns the rice yellow and adds authentic flavor.

Desserts

You can use 1 or 2 different berries instead of 3; simply keep the amount of berries the same.

Three Berry Crisp

8–10 servings

1 pound ripe strawberries, sliced

3 pints of blueberries

2 pints raspberries

½ cup sugar

Juice of 1 lemon

½ teaspoon ground nutmeg

2 sticks butter, divided

½ cup flour

1 cup brown sugar packed

Pinch of salt

1¼ cup uncooked oatmeal

1 recipe Spicy Hot Fudge Sauce, Chapter 10, or whipped cream

1. Preheat oven to 375°F. Grease a 9" or 10" pie plate.

2. Melt ½ stick of butter; set aside.

3. In a large bowl, mix together berries, sugar, lemon, nutmeg, and the ½ stick melted butter. Put berry mixture into prepared pie plate.

4. Cut the remaining 1½ sticks of butter into pieces. Add them to a food processor along with the flour, brown sugar, salt, and uncooked oatmeal until coarsely blended. (You can also use a fork or pastry cutter to mix together the ingredients.)

5. Top berries with crisp mixture and bake for 35–45 minutes. It's done when the berries are bubbling, the oatmeal mixture is a golden color, and your entire house smells terrific!

6. Serve warm with whipped cream or Spicy Hot Fudge Sauce, Chapter 10.

Hot Fudge Bacon Sundae

Serves 4

4 chocolate brownies (see Bittersweet Brownies, Chapter 10)

2 small ripe bananas (optional)

1 pint of your favorite chocolate ice cream

1 cup hot fudge sauce, or Spicy Hot Fudge Sauce, Chapter 10

Whipped cream

2 strips bacon, cooked and crumbled

Top each brownie with half of a banana (if desired), 2 scoops of chocolate ice cream, hot fudge sauce, and whipped cream. Garnish with crispy bacon pieces and serve immediately.

Floating Clouds

Makes 2

½ cup milk

½ cup half-and-half or cream

2–3 shots amaretto liqueur (my preference is Disaronno)

½ cup ice

Whipped cream

Cinnamon or nutmeg to taste

Add milk, cream, amaretto, and ice to a blender and blend until smooth. Pour into glasses and top each with whipped cream and cinnamon or nutmeg.

Chocolate Mousse

Serves 4

6 ounces baking chocolate, broken into squares

2 tablespoons butter, cut into 4 pieces

4 egg whites (used pasteurized eggs if you prefer)

Pinch of salt

¼ teaspoon vanilla extract

1 cup heavy cream

Dark or white chocolate shavings for garnish, optional

1. Put chocolate in microwave-safe dish and heat in the microwave on high for 1 minute, 30 seconds, then stir. Repeat in 30-second intervals until chocolate is almost entirely melted.

2. Add butter. Heat in microwave for another 30 seconds until both ingredients are melted. Stir to mix. Set aside and let cool for 10 minutes.

3. Beat egg whites and salt together till stiff foam forms.

4. In a separate bowl, whisk cream and vanilla until thick.

5. Add chocolate-butter mixture to egg whites in thirds until mixed.

6. Add chocolate-egg white mixture to cream mixture and mix.

7. Place in serving bowls (I like to use martini glasses!) and chill for 1 hour.

8. Serve with dark or white chocolate shavings.

Gypsy Gourmet

For a special treat, use white chocolate baking squares and add 2 tablespoons crème de cacao (white chocolate liqueur) after the butter and chocolate are melted.

 For best results, use Ghirardelli or Callebaut chocolate.

Bittersweet Brownies with Spicy Hot Fudge Sauce

Serves 6–8

8–9 ounces bittersweet chocolate, broken into pieces

2 sticks butter

1¾ cups all-purpose flour

1 teaspoon baking powder

½ teaspoon salt

4 eggs

2 cups sugar

2 teaspoons vanilla extract

1 cup chopped walnuts, plus a few whole walnuts for topping (optional)

1 recipe Spicy Hot Fudge Sauce, Chapter 10

Gypsy Gourmet

For a special flavor, add 2 tablespoons Tia Maria coffee liqueur from Jamaica with the butter and chocolate and melt together.

1. Preheat oven to 350°F.

2. Grease 9" baking pan and set aside.

3. In microwave-safe bowl, melt butter and chocolate on high in 30 second intervals. Set aside.

4. In a large bowl, mix flour, baking powder, and salt. Set aside.

5. In another bowl, whisk together eggs, sugar, and vanilla.

6. Slowly fold chocolate mixture into egg mixture till blended.

7. Add chocolate-egg mixture into flour mixture. Mix thoroughly. If adding walnuts, incorporate them into batter.

8. Place mixture in greased pan. Toss a few whole walnuts on top of batter, if desired.

9. Bake for 40–45 minutes. Cool. Serve over vanilla or chocolate ice cream with Spicy Hot Fudge Sauce, Chapter 10, and whipped cream.

Spicy Hot Fudge Sauce

Makes one cup

1 cup hot fudge sauce or chocolate sauce of your choice

⅛ teaspoon habanero pepper powder or cayenne pepper

1. Mix ingredients together in a microwave-safe container.

2. Heat covered on high for 1–2 minutes. Stir.

3. Serve over Bittersweet Brownies, Chapter 10, ice cream, and chocolate cake.

Gypsy Gourmet

To make this treat extra-special, substitute:

- Amaretti di Saronno Cookies for the regular sugar cookies

- 3 tablespoons mascarpone cheese for the whipped cream

- 1½ tablespoons Chocolate Vincotto dolcé nero sauce for the Spicy Hot Fudge Sauce

Strawberry-Sugar Cookie Crumb

1 serving

2–3 sugar cookies, crushed

3 tablespoons whipped cream

3–4 large strawberries, sliced

1½ tablespoons Spicy Hot Fudge Sauce, Chapter 10

1. Line small bowl or dessert cup with cookies and top with whipped cream, then strawberries.

2. Drizzle hot fudge sauce over the top.

Toasted Almond Banana Treat

Makes 6 desserts

5 large, very ripe bananas

1½ cups whipped cream

1 teaspoon almond extract

Pinch of salt

1 tablespoon sugar

2 tablespoons slivered toasted almonds

1. Mash bananas or put through sieve into bowl.

2. Add whipped cream, almond extract, salt, and sugar.

3. Divide mashed banana mixture into six small serving bowls. Sprinkle with almonds.

Pineapple Tulip Cups

Makes 3

8 ounces fruit jam, your preference

Whipped cream to your taste

2 8-ounce cans of crushed pineapple, drained

9 lady finger cookies

1. Line a martini glass or small margarita glass with lady fingers (3 per glass).

2. Place 1 tablespoon of jam at bottom of each glass. Then layer pineapple, whipped cream, and jam in several layers.

3. Chill for one hour.

4. Top with final layer of a tall whipped cream swirl when ready to serve.

Gypsy Gourmet

For a different take on this recipe, use mascarpone cheese instead of fruit jam.

INDEX